Sell Your Story in a
Single Sentence

Sell Your Story in a Single Sentence

Advice from the
Front Lines of Hollywood

Lane Shefter Bishop

THE COUNTRYMAN PRESS
A division of W. W. Norton & Company
Independent Publishers Since 1923

Printed in the United States of America

For information about permission to reproduce selections from this book, write to Permissions, The Countryman Press, 500 Fifth Avenue, New York, NY 10110

For information about special discounts for bulk purchases, please contact W. W. Norton Special Sales at specialsales@wwnorton.com or 800-233-4830

Manufacturing by Edwards Brothers Malloy
Book design by Brian Mulligan

978-1-58157-368-8

The Countryman Press
www.countrymanpress.com

A division of W. W. Norton & Company
500 Fifth Avenue, New York, NY 10110
www.wwnorton.com

1 2 3 4 5 6 7 8 9 0

I'd like to dedicate this book to my
husband, Andrew, who—since the day we
met—has given me the gift of supporting
me wholeheartedly in absolutely
everything I pursue.

Contents

The Value of
a Logline

"WHAT'S YOUR STORY ABOUT?"

It's the million-dollar question that writers—screenwriters, authors, really anyone putting pen to paper—whether just starting out or highly experienced, get asked perpetually during their long creation process. When faced with this situation, most writers do one of three things: One, they stare blankly, like a deer in headlights, grasping for words that will adequately describe their baby even as they realize they have not in any way prepared for this critical moment. Two, they try to create a 'tease' or 'surprise' in response by dutifully reciting their back-cover blurb, which unfortunately serves to make their masterpiece sound terribly generic. The last resort is to stumble through a painfully long-winded plot description that includes an excessive amount of unnecessary information and sucks up a great deal of time—boring the listener to distraction.

What's needed is a top-notch logline, a one-line selling tool like no other. It's a writer's most important asset—invaluable for query letters, for keeping laser-focused on what makes a story unique, and for having the perfect elevator pitch ready to go. By learning the secret to writing the best logline possible, a content creator can literally sell their story in a single sentence. This book is the key to unlocking that potential.

In the Beginning . . .

AS A PRODUCER IN HOLLYWOOD, I LEARNED EARLY ON the value of being able to sell something in a sentence. Most execs just don't have time to hear an endless plot description, nor read 300 pages of a manuscript. Screenwriters would complain to me about how hard it was to get anyone to read just a 120-page script, but when I asked what their screenplay was about, I was told "It's *Jaws* meets *The Mosquito Coast*" or "It's *Memoirs of a Geisha* meets *The Soloist*." Those slap-dash descriptions could fit many screenplays from many screenwriters. So how does that help you sell your specific story? The simple answer is that it doesn't.

During my two-year stint as an executive vice president on the buying side, I would have sincerely appreciated someone who could swiftly and concisely tell me about their project. It would have saved legions of unnecessary meetings and gruelingly long phone calls. Sometimes just getting to the heart of a story was a painful process—but without that knowledge, how could I sell it to a studio or network? As a result, many hours of my job became the struggle to design a logline for properties in our slate when the actual creator had no idea how to sell his or her own piece.

When I started my own company, Vast Entertainment, I decided to focus solely on literary material rather than scripts. I knew from experience that if 200 screenplays arrived as incoming submissions, maybe two of them were good. But if two hundred books came in, probably 50 to a 100 of them could provide a nice base for a film or television project. It was a matter of a higher rate of return for my reading hours. Yet I was in for a rude awakening.

At that time, I found that no one wanted to hear about what they considered "lengthy material." The page count didn't even matter: Books as a whole just seemed too daunting. It was all the buying executives could do to focus on shorter, more concise screenplays; they certainly didn't have the extensive free time to read multiple novels. You'd practically hear a groan when you mentioned that the project was based on a book, and you just knew they were going to make some poor 19-year-old intern read it instead and deliver a short write-up on the plot. I vividly remember one executive literally starting to rearrange items on his desk instead of even pretending to listen, once I mentioned my pitch was based on a book. So it became abundantly clear to me that I had to change my approach if I wanted to set anything up.

I became fixated on the idea of simply focusing on what made a property unique and how I could make that element very clear, very fast, with the most dramatic punch I could muster. After all, everyone wants something that feels fresh, shiny, and new, right? Soon, and with a great deal of struggle as well as a ridiculous amount of trial and error, I determined the concept and elements of a true logline. And I began to sell, setting up more than twenty projects in the first two years through a steady stream of pitches and meetings. With this nod to success, I thought that I couldn't possibly be the only one looking for this manna from heaven. So for the last few years I've traveled all across the country, and even internationally, speaking at writers' conferences, screenwriting events, authors' workshops, and book conventions about crafting the amazing selling tool of the perfect logline.

By traveling far and wide, I discovered that the need for this information is, in fact, huge. I speak to thousands of content creators each year who all have questions about how to pitch their material, how to create a selling sentence, how to determine the heart of their work, and how to specify what makes it truly distinctive in an inundated marketplace. And they are from all experience levels, the novice to the professional, and from all walks of life. Literally hundreds of "help me" logline queries are fielded by my offices monthly.

A writer once started a pitch by saying to me, "I know you've probably heard many people today telling you their fantasy stories . . ." I stopped him right there and said, "Why don't you start by telling me what makes your story unique from the other hundred tales in the same genre I've heard today?" That, of course, is the crux of the logline.

There's never been a book on the art of crafting a true one-sentence logline and the timing is perfect, because films like Twilight, The Hunger Games, and especially Harry Potter really opened the doors for book-to-film adaptations to take center stage. In fact, in the last five years, 16 out of 35 (or about 45 percent) of the Academy Award Best Picture-nominated films were all based on books. In 2014 alone, 31 feature films that were originally novels came out in theaters.

It's no surprise, since many books already possess a huge built-in following, which usually translates well into box-office dollars. *Insurgent* alone grabbed $52.3 million in its opening weekend at the US box office, just shy of *Divergent*'s $54.6 million debut. The *Divergent* franchise, based on teen action books by Veronica Roth, has garnered a plump $388 million so far, with two movies still to come. According to *Forbes*, nearly a quarter of the 200 top-grossing films worldwide tallied by Box Office Mojo have been directly adapted from books. Today, astonishingly, nearly 50 percent of all films made are derived from some type of previous piece of work—comics/graphic novels, articles, books, magazines, short stories, and the like. So having underlying material or IP (intellectual property) is now a much-desired resource and can literally be the difference between making the sale and leaving empty-handed.

For example, I have a property about a sociopath lawyer. (I know, some say those are synonyms.) But even with an A-list screenwriter coming in and pitching their fantastic idea for a new sociopath lawyer show, I couldn't sell it if I couldn't also say, "It's based on an amazing book about a real lawyer, in her 30s and attractive, who is currently living in California, teaching law students, and who literally tested in the 99th percentile for sociopathy." Suddenly, it's not just made-up fodder from the writers' minds—it truly exists in reality, and by being based on underlying material, the story becomes infinitely more marketable.

Many times, screenwriters tell me that they are having trouble selling their screenplays and ask me if I think they should write a book built on the story they've created. My answer is always the same—a universal "yes." Basing a script on literary material makes it a more sellable property these days. And many times, the process of creating the logline for the book helps refocus the writer on what problems were inherent in their screenplay that they didn't see before. Sometimes, I also recommend that they look for news articles online that would support their story, if they need underlying IP and cannot find the right book. You can always find pieces that have to do with one component or another in the script, and those can become your "inspired by" elements. The more ammunition the better in this flooded marketplace—and underlying material, no matter what the source, will make the screenplay even more valuable.

I'm considered a bit of an anomaly in the industry. First of all, because I am a book-to-screen *only* producer, which means every single one of my projects starts as a book property. And second of all, because I now focus solely on setting up literary material very, very early. In fact, my whole business plan for Vast Entertainment shifted when I realized that I didn't have to wait for a full manuscript in order to set up film or television deals for literary properties. Sometimes it's even easier to sell without it, because then the buyer doesn't have as many reasons to say no— the book isn't even finished being written yet. It's sort of like reverse engineering: I can say to the buyer, "What doesn't work for you about the material? I can have the author change it, since it's still in process." Today, about 85% of the material I set up for film and television is either only a simple book proposal or a short partial (approximately 50 to 100 pages), and as far as I know, I'm the only one working in this fashion in the industry today.

Luckily, I can undertake this different type of business model specifically because I am blessed enough to have special relationships with the literary agents I work with in New York—currently about sixty of them. Over the years, I've built up a trust level with them, and because of this, they feel comfortable sending me material very early in the process, many times before any publisher has seen a single page. That trust comes from the fact that, based on experience, they know that I'm not going to paper the town with their babies nor take it to any buyer without permission. (Unfortunately, there are many producers who do shop material they don't have permission to be trying to sell.) Also, on occasion, I am able to return the favor by helping them navigate an option deal or finding out if a producer who has contacted them is legitimate.

I've even been fortunate enough to get calls from agents such as this one: "My author just pitched me three ideas and I had her write up 20 pages on each one. Do you mind checking them out and seeing which you think is most marketable to the entertainment industry?"

Of course I said yes, and in fact, I ended up setting up one of those books with Ineffable Pictures. We have just partnered on it with Joel Silver's company—not too bad for a project that started out with only 20 pages. The funny thing is that it was the only idea the agent felt should be shelved, and had told the writer to backburner it. Instead, I told the agent to have the woman start writing the full story out immediately. It was very high-concept and very marketable—all about a world where organic items have been replaced by synthetics, electronics, and technology. Food is obsolete and the protagonist starts to get hungry—which is illegal . . .

I also believe in treating people well, which is sometimes—sadly—a rarity in this industry. I email or write back to all of the agents I work with as quickly as possible. I give them continuous emailed updates on the status of their properties, and I never take anything anywhere without explicit permission—period. Anything they've asked me to keep to myself, I do. I also make sure to travel to New York as much as possible, because there is nothing like a face-to-face coffee instead of a voice over the phone. In fact, *The DUFF*, which came out as a feature film in early 2015, is the first literary property I ever set up, and I only got it early because I was literally sitting in the agent's office when the rough draft came in to her email inbox. She'd already had a multitude of calls from interns and assistants at various companies requesting copies of the manuscript, based on the Publishers Marketplace announcement, but I was there in person, excited to read it, and passionate about my ability to set it up—which I did by packaging with McG's company and CBS Films. To clarify, McG is a big producer and I brought the book, *The DUFF*, to his company, Wonderland Sound and Vision, in order to have a strong producing partner. Ultimately, Lionsgate came on board to distribute the picture. In this instance, the book basically sold itself, because the title means "Designated Ugly Fat Friend"—which was a great built-in selling tool—but that is a real rarity. Nine times out of ten, you have to be able to market the book or whatever the underlying IP is yourself, and that's done by crafting a first-rate logline.

Truly, the most important commodity in the film industry, as with most industries, is time—because no one has any. We are all running around crazily with our iPads and iPhones, hopping planes or trains, trying to cram in "just one more thing" in order to try to make a living and reduce the size of our to-do lists. So the only way to get people excited about a property, whether book or script, idea or invention, is to grab their attention and grab it quickly. Because no matter how busy people are, they always have time to hear one sentence. In all honesty, this lesson became the most valuable one I've learned in my numerous years in the entertainment business. And now, I'm passing the result of that insight—the art of the logline—along to you.

CHAPTER 1

What is
a Logline?

AS A PRODUCER IN THE ENTERTAINMENT INDUSTRY, I am constantly selling. I sell literary agents on the idea of bringing me a "sneak peek" look at early-stage material—book proposals and partials—prior to it going out to publishers. I sell network and studio executives as well as A-list independent producers on the excitement of new properties coming down the pike—especially those not yet in a publisher's hands. Most importantly, I sell the network and studio development folks on what these projects *could* be—a TV series, a movie of the week, a mini-series, or full-length feature motion picture, based on the literary material. How do I do all of this? With a perfect logline—a one-sentence selling tool like no other.

A logline is literally what will sell your material—a powerfully crafted single sentence that highlights what is most unique about your work. With a perfect logline, you can emphasize how what you have created is different from what anyone else has, and thus help yourself immensely by showing others why they should want what you have.

A few years ago, after spending countless hours creating loglines from the material I was receiving, it occurred to me that it would be extremely helpful (as well as save me a great deal of time) if the writers themselves could provide a logline for their material to their agents—who, in turn, could pass them along to me. So I made this request and, to my utter surprise, received anything but loglines. They were either an amalgamation of the back-cover blurb and a synopsis, or an extremely long run-on sentence trying to incorporate the entire plot. "Don't these writers use loglines at the top of their query letters?" I asked. "Don't agents use them to pitch editors and publishers?"

"Yes," came the reply—these hot-mess write-ups were it. That's when I realized content creators needed help, and lots of it. I knew firsthand that there was a top-notch marketing tool available to help them instantly sell their work, if they only knew how to do it. And that's when my numerous seminars, speaking engagements, webinars, and, ultimately, this book sparked to life.

So what is a logline? Well, in the simplest terms, it's the answer to the question "What's your story about?" It helps content creators simply and easily sell their work in a single sentence, because the emphasis is on what makes their property unique. In business, it's called the "elevator pitch," because it can be said in the time it takes to get from one floor to another while standing with someone in an elevator. The best part of that one line, of course, is that if done correctly, it can entice someone to read your full material—which is always the ultimate goal.

Specifically, the logline provides the content creator with a concise way to focus on the three main anchors of their writing:

Who is the protagonist?
What do they want?
What is at stake?

Most importantly, creating a logline involves figuring out the most unique answers to those questions. By carefully defining and solidifying these three elements and what makes them distinctive early on in the process (by creating a successful logline), the content creator can save hours of rewriting later on down the line. I often say that the logline is sort of like a rudder on a boat—keeping writers on course to where they are going as they weave their tales. Just as you wouldn't sail a ship without a rudder, you shouldn't write out your material in full without a logline. Clearly, the payoff is that a successful logline not only sells the creative work upon completion, it also keeps the creator inexorably on-point throughout the process. That's why I always tell people to try to design their logline first, while they are fleshing out what they want to write, and then get started on the bulk of their masterpiece.

In order to further define what a logline is, let's take a moment to explore what it is not. First and foremost, let me start by tackling a standard misconception. A logline is not the recitation of one film title meets another film title. This blank-meets-blank shorthand was developed years ago by studio execs in order to pitch their bosses on high-concept films they wanted green-lit. It has since been adopted by others as an uber-quick selling tool but, let me reiterate, this format is *not* a logline. Personally, I don't even understand how saying something is *"Fantastic Four meets 2001: A Space Odyssey,"* for example, helps you sell your specific story. First of all, it says absolutely nothing about your particular piece. Secondly, by referencing those movies you are assuming that the listener knows exactly what you mean by your comparisons, though in actuality there's a big window for misinterpretation. What if they think you mean your project is like those two films because of the characters, and you actually meant the association to relate to the tone of the film or films? Also, if the listener hasn't seen one of those movies, you really haven't helped yourself at all. Lastly, in this type of scenario, you are usually referencing features that did really well in the theater in order to get the listener's excitement up. By doing that, you've raised the bar extremely high right away, and that's a lot for your personal project to live up to.

Next, a logline is *not* the back-cover blurb. That write-up is often intentionally vague and only hints as to what the reader can expect the tale to be about. It's usually a sneak peek at what's inside the pages of the work. The problem with this "tease" is that it makes the story sound terribly generic, since the specifics of a journey are what make it different. For example, many stories could be classified as "a mother/daughter tale in which they learn to fix their broken relationship through a difficult experience." That boring description covers a large number of written works, I am sure. But if we learn instead that the mentally disturbed daughter nearly dies from some rare disease that the mom can miraculously fix by giving her own blood to her previously estranged child, it begins to distinguish itself from the other mother/daughter tales. Think about it—how can your story stand out from other properties in the exact same genre if you don't let your reader know what specifically makes it unique?

Many writers, when told to be much more specific, tell me that they don't want to "spoil it" by "giving it away." I always ask them, "Why not? Why not share with everyone the coolest part of your story?" That's the way to get someone to actually read it. Here's an example: If I tell you my story is about a gardener who has exceptional abilities, you may be a little bit interested. But if I tell you that my story is about a gardener with magical powers who can influence all wildlife to grow into living artwork, you are sure to be much more intrigued. Additionally, if you tease me with familiar generalities, I will most likely feel like I've already read many other similar stories, so why should I bother reading yours? And that's definitely not the reaction you want as a content creator.

Let me also clarify that a logline is not what you see written on movie posters. Those little blurbs are typically meant to be a kind of a tease that hints at there being something fun or cool or interesting about the project; the goal is to entice you into wanting to go see the film. Think about *Titanic*, for example. The poster reads: "Nothing on Earth Could Come Between Them." Does that actually tell you anything at all about the epic love story? Not at all. *Dirty Dancing* reads: "The Time of Your Life." Of course, nothing in those five words in any way indicates what the film is about. For *Dumb and Dumber*, the blurb is: "For Harry and Lloyd, Every Day is a No-Brainer," which—while very cute—again, doesn't tell you about the story itself. Those blurbs on the posters may help in the studio marketing team meeting, but they are not in any way loglines.

Next, let me make it abundantly clear that a logline is *not* a retelling of the entire plot, crammed into one very long run-on sentence. You'd be surprised at how many writers try desperately to make that work, to no avail. I've seen some supposed loglines that were absolutely ridiculous: lengthy sentences with dashes and parentheses and all manner of cheats to try to make a one-liner. Aside from the fact that it's virtually impossible to cram a creative and detailed story into one sentence, why would you want to? If you tell the reader every single thing that happens in your piece, then they don't need to read your work, and that's the exact response you don't want.

Instead, a logline is one sentence that shines a spotlight on the most unique part of your tale—the part that will make someone say, "I want to read that." Those are the golden words that a successful logline can achieve for you. This book will put you directly and firmly on that path. So let's start by looking at the three most important questions involved in beginning the creation of the perfect logline.

CHAPTER 2

Who is the Protagonist?

WHO IS THE PROTAGONIST? FOR A WRITER, THIS SEEMS like the most basic of questions. Sometimes, at writers' conferences, I even get a chuckle from the audience when I bring up this topic. And yet, so many times, writers tell me their entire plot in frustration—not being able to create a solid logline—and I'll point out that the person or people in their logline don't seem to be the ones driving the story forward. Suddenly, understanding dawns. While these other characters may be important, they should not be the focus of the logline. None of them are the protagonist.

Often, a character can be a favorite, fabulous in their own right, and thus seemingly important to both writer and plot, but that character is not actually the one motivating the journey and moving the story along from point A to point B to point C. This is difficult for some content creators to understand, because they are jumping ahead to ideas like how cool a character would be if that role were played by a well-known A-list actor, or how much fun that particular character is to write because of a great sense of humor, or no conscience to speak of, or a razor-sharp wit. Those are all things that may be true, but they still don't make that character the grounded center of the logline.

Sometimes, the toughest thing for writers is that they fall in love with their own material. So for them, every character is important to the story—and in the literary work itself, that's completely valid. But for our purposes, it's all about defining who is continuously driving the story onward, which character's actions are the plot points hinging upon, and who is making decisions that end in scenarios of risk, revealing what's at stake. Answer these questions and you have your logline's protagonist.

Here's an example of a logline that had to tackle this particular demon before it could be created properly.

ORIGINAL

A man discovers that abandoned hospitals are actually time portals and that he can travel to the past and change whatever he wants, but when his assistant finds out what he's doing, he realizes he has to go back and change things enough to make her disappear.

As you can tell, when I was first brought this story, the content creator thought that the boss character was the protagonist, since he was actively adjusting things in time—and the stilted logline the writer had created reflected that. However, in working through the logline and discussing the full plot, it became clear that the woman—the assistant—was actually the lead character in terms of the logline. She was the one with desperate stakes, which motivated her journey: After all, if she didn't succeed in stopping her boss then her own existence would be wiped out. Here's the redone version, prior to any vocabulary tweaking and/or finessing:

REDO

A woman procuring abandoned hospitals discovers they're time portals her boss is using to change the past, and must stop him before he erases her existence.

Now, in this iteration, with the real protagonist defined, we truly feel what's at stake, and the urgency of the journey comes through loud and clear. That boss character is obviously important to the story: In fact, he's the antagonist. But in logline creation, it's important to stay focused on the protagonist, because the protagonist is the one who has something to lose if the journey is not completed in a satisfying way. The protagonist reveals to the reader the most important element and driving force in any story—what is truly at stake.

I find it funny now that the writer and I spent so many hours crafting this logline with the female assistant as the lead, since we ended up drastically changing it later. An executive I deal with at Universal Pictures loved the story but not the female lead, because most of their action-based films have a male in the main role. So the writer and I went back to the drawing board and created a new logline with the initial time jumper—a male mercenary—as the lead (since the boss lets that guy do the first, more dangerous jumps). Of course, the final book manuscript was ultimately adjusted to match. Here's a draft of the redone logline:

A mercenary performing time jumps via "haunted" hospitals must stop his boss from using the portals to change the past before the man erases his existence.

Notice that the female assistant has been completely removed from the logline. That's because, for our purposes, she is no longer the protagonist, and therefore an unnecessary element. The initial time jumper/mercenary has now taken on that role. You can see from this example how important it was to define the protagonist first. With the original, rather confused, antagonist-based logline, we could have never successfully made the switch from the female lead to the male lead character's perspective, as the buyer requested, because the protagonist wasn't at the forefront.

Here's another project I had for which the writer provided a logline that focused on the wrong person/people:

ORIGINAL

Three half-angels struggle to protect a half-angel/half-human girl from the devil because it's the only way to keep the balance between good and evil.

While the concept of half-angels is definitely a cool one, their journey of protecting someone to keep the balance between the amorphous "good" and "evil" just isn't that exciting. In fact, except for the half-angel concept, it sounds kind of generic, overall. I know from experience that this can happen when the writer has focused on the wrong lead character(s). For our logline purposes, the half-angels are not the protagonists. (We'll delve into the multiple protagonists issue in just a bit.) I spoke to the writer to get more specifics about the good and evil part of the story and find out why the devil would want this girl in particular—what was at stake. Here's the redone rough draft logline:

REDO
A half-angel/half-human girl, who's the last bit of good-ness in the world, must destroy the devil or all evil will be unleashed from hell.

If you go back and read the original logline, you'll see that there is a pretty big difference. That's because the girl is actually the protagonist, not the other half-angels, which was made clear to me by the fact that simply protecting someone isn't a very active role, so they couldn't be the protagonists. It's now crystal clear that it's the girl's much bigger and much more risk-filled journey that we care about—especially now, because the stakes regarding evil taking over the world are more clearly defined. As you'll find me reiterating many times throughout this book, you can never go wrong by being more specific.

The other reason that defining the protagonist is so important is that this component can play an important role in the market-ability of your material. I was at a meeting recently at Paramount Television, what's commonly referred to as a "meet and greet." During the meeting, I got to know the executive and he got to know me, but more important, he let me know what types of material the company was looking for. The interesting thing was that the exec defined the different genres they wanted to explore (noir, action, et cetera), but he also emphasized that every project had to have a really interesting character as its base. So, in essence, his interest was less about the type of show (or even the storyline) and more about what type of person was at its core, moving the action along. That protagonist essentially defined the series for him; that's what he concentrated on in terms of sparking interest. That was great information to have, because then I was able to pitch him a property with a fabulously complex character at its center, starting with the logline, of course. That led to the immediate request for me to email over my full write-up—exactly the response I was hoping for.

Okay, so step number one is determining who the protagonist is. As you've seen, while this is a deceptively simple question, it does not always have a simple answer. Now that you have that concept down, I'm going to shake things up a bit. In Hollywood, we call this "throwing rocks" at the character—making everything more difficult.

What do you do if you think you have two protagonists in your story instead of only one?

Chapter 3

What If There Are Two Protagonists?

OCCASIONALLY, I GET ASKED ABOUT HOW TO HANDLE stories told by two protagonists, or material that involves alternating narrators. More often than not in this situation, the content creator thinks there is more than one protagonist when there is really only one. Just because every other chapter in the story is told by a different speaker doesn't always mean that there are two central characters with regards to the logline. As a writer, you may need both perspectives to tell your tale the way it needs to be told, but those narrators aren't necessarily dual protagonists, for our purposes.

Here's an example of a submitted logline where the content creator felt that his story had two protagonists:

ORIGINAL

A boy and his brother inadvertently discover the ghost of a murdered blind girl, and the two must prove who did it so justice can be done.

I spent quite a bit of time asking the writer if the brother was just as integral to the story as the boy himself: Did they both explore the locations together? Discover the girl together? Eventually, it became clear that while they did pursue much of the plot in tandem, it was really the original boy making the decisions about when they did what and how. The brother was there only because it turned out that their mother was actually the killer (and, by the way, that's a nifty revelation that should be solidly included in the logline itself). In the end, the brother is not one of two protagonists in our logline because he's not making the choices which move the story forward. Here's the rough redo:

REDO

A boy discovers the ghost of a murdered blind girl and must prove his own mother was the killer.

Notice that, with one of the two brothers removed, the sentence has more focus and power. Always remember: It's never as interesting if two people are doing the exact same thing. By taking one away, you have just streamlined and defined who your audience should care about, be rooting for, and want to follow on the journey. This clean and clear understanding is an important element in connecting with readers, getting their attention, and keeping it. Since that is your ultimate goal, why not use everything at your disposal to help make it happen?

I have a project in development that's a story about Typhoid Mary, the first person in the US who carried Typhoid Fever and infected 51 people before being forcibly quarantined. The book, which is still being written, currently has both Mary and the girl she's after (a descendant of a man who did her wrong) as alternating narrators. While this works in the manuscript, it definitely won't work for our logline purposes. In this case, as with most, two narrators do not in any way mean that there are two leads. So the question becomes: Who is the protagonist for the logline?

First instinct might tell you that it is Typhoid Mary, since she's the main subject of the spooky tale. But we had to ask ourselves: Do Mary's decisions move the story along? Is she the one with high stakes? The answer is no. It's the girl she's after. That girl decides to go out with her friends to a scary island. There, she decides to explore dilapidated buildings. Her ancestry brings the wrath of Mary upon her, and it's her life that is at stake if she does not defeat Typhoid Mary. So the girl is our protagonist and Mary is actually our antagonist. Here's the rough draft logline:

A girl discovers that Typhoid Mary is alive, seeking vengeance upon her, and must find a way to escape the woman's deadly island.

As you can see, while Mary is without a doubt an important part of the logline, there is only one protagonist here: the girl who must flee to save her own skin. She is the one who has something to lose if she fails—her life.

Recently, I was asked about the musical *Wicked*, which the writer thought was a good example of a story with two protagonists. During the course of the musical, both Glinda and Elphaba feel like they have equal stage time. However, for log-

line purposes, I would say that there is actually only one protagonist. Why? Because it is Elphaba who is truly taking us on her
journey. She's the one who changes the most, and has to learn
the lesson that trying to adjust herself to be someone she's not
will never serve her. It is her character arc, consisting of coming
into her own and accepting herself for who she really is, which
propels the plot of the story forward throughout the musical.
Glinda is just helping her along.

Of course, there are exceptions to every rule. There are indeed
stories where there are truly two protagonists—and sometimes
they *are* told in alternating chapters. For this scenario to be the
case, the two protagonists must be essentially equal in every
way. In other words, both characters have to learn just as much
through their journey as well as equally motivate the story along
its path, while revealing what's at stake for each of them. Here's
an example of a logline with two equal protagonists:

*A man and his sworn enemy must learn to become best
friends, to survive being stranded on a dangerous island.*

Here, both characters are given equal time in the manuscript and are essentially two halves of the same whole story.
Also, they have exactly opposite actions and reactions: What
one does affects the other. (Neither of them is the antagonist.
The island itself takes on that role, because it's the dangers
inherent there that both of the men have to overcome.) So this
unusual story is an exception to the rule, and the logline does
indeed indicate two distinct protagonists. I must emphasize,
however, that this exact equality between two characters is

truly unusual, and most stories have one protagonist for logline purposes.

Here's yet another scenario for you to think about: While most stories have one protagonist, and every once in a while there's a story that really does have two protagonists, what if you are dealing with a story with many characters, making up an ensemble? What if you feel that there are *multiple* protagonists in your story?

Chapter 4

The Group
Perspective

I'VE BEEN ASKED IF THERE COULD EVER BE A GROUP OF protagonists in what most people would consider an ensemble story. Usually the answer is no. Even if a group of people are along for a particular journey, typically there is always one who is leading the others from event to event based on his or her decisions. Think about *Guardians of the Galaxy*, for instance. Peter Quill may have Rocket, Groot, and Gamora all together as an unusual quartet on their crazy adventure, but *he* is the one motivating the action. *His* choices propel the movie along through its two-plus hours. It's the same with *The Wizard of Oz*. The Lion, the Tin Man, and the Scarecrow are all along on Dorothy's journey—she is the protagonist because it is her desire to get home that propels the story forward. She will be the one trapped without her aunt and uncle if she can't make it out of Oz and back to their farm in Kansas.

One of the many jobs of the logline is to simplify the throughline or main plot for the audience so that understanding the main selling point of the property is easy to discern. If there are multiple protagonists then that job becomes extremely difficult, if not impossible. Therefore, most of the time, even if there are multiple points of view in the story, the logline can be streamlined to focus only on one lead character (or possibly two, as mentioned in the previous chapter). This is, of course, done simply by asking the questions I posed earlier about whose choices are truly moving the action forward to its conclusion and who has something to lose if he or she fails in reaching whatever the goal is.

That said: Once again, there are exceptions to every rule. One that comes to mind is *The Big Bang Theory*, which is a true ensemble show. Each episode focuses on a different one of the guys in their smart group of four. If Sheldon and/or Leonard were the only protagonist(s), that would be a different situation, but there are just as many episodes about Howard's mother and Raj's perpetual girlfriend search, etc., so the overall show has four equal protagonists. Here's a very rough draft logline to show how to deal with that situation:

Four geniuses learn from their hot blonde neighbor that there is more to life and love than just science.

All four of the guys acquire knowledge from Penny, either directly or indirectly (through her on-again, off-again relationship with Leonard), that they would never have gotten had they forsaken her friendship and stayed only within their tight group of four. Each week, a different lesson is learned by one of these main characters. Again, this is truly the exception to the rule. In normal circumstances, for most TV programs and feature films, this group protagonist approach does not apply.

Another exception to the rule would be the Garry Marshall romantic comedy film *Valentine's Day*. The movie follows a group of different characters and their struggles with regard to both love and the Valentine's Day holiday. All of the main characters in this ensemble piece get fairly equal screen time and their individual journeys get equal weight through interconnecting stories within the overall feature. Because of this, the logline would again require the group perspective. It might be something like this:

A group of interrelated characters struggle through makeups and breakups due to the pressures associated with Valentine's Day.

It still needs work, but the necessity for a multiple-protagonist perspective is clear.

I was asked recently about a logline for *Game of Thrones* (my absolute favorite series on TV right now), and I think that show is the most unusual of all exceptions. The fact that many of the protagonists die in the course of George R. R. Martin's book series means that creating a logline must necessarily include a group perspective. This is because the protagonists keep changing; as one gets killed, another takes his or her place. It's a very uncommon but fascinating scenario. Creating the logline for *Game of Thrones* was a difficult and, believe me, time-consuming process, but since I am always talking about how absolutely anything can be broken down into a solid logline, I was determined to prove that one could be crafted, even with this kind of rare material that has an ever-changing roster of protagonists. My rough draft version looked like this:

> *Leaders of the Seven Kingdoms fight each other to the death through strategic, bloody, and dragon-filled civil wars, with the goal of becoming "King of the Iron Throne."*

The leaders make up the group of protagonists because *Game of Thrones* is one of only a handful of book series I know in which most of the main characters die fairly early on and are replaced by others. This is very unusual, however, and I must reiterate that this is a very rare exception to the rule. Nine times out of ten, there is only one solid protagonist for a true logline.

Now that we've explored one, two, and even multiple protagonist examples, we finally know *who* is driving the story forwards. Now we need to determine what is motivating their journey. In other words, what does the protagonist truly want?

Chapter 5

What Does
the Protagonist
Want?

THE SIMPLE QUESTION OF WHAT THE PROTAGONIST desires, not emotionally but in a solid and concrete fashion, stumps so many writers that I am continuously perplexed by how they can have written a full manuscript without this knowledge firmly cemented in their minds. After all, the main character's desire is what provides the motivation for the journey that person is on throughout the story. It is what propels them forward as well as what instills urgency and pressure. In Hollywood, we call this force "the ticking clock." Without this, the protagonist becomes extremely passive, a pawn tossed to and fro from event to event, and these incidents then have no emotional resonance. That is because the character is moving through the story with no particular direction and without active participation in his or her own fate. When a story feels like it has no pacing, it is often because there isn't a ticking clock.

Many times, when I ask about what a character wants, writers give me grand emotional beats, huge generalizations which range from "he wants to find true love" to "she wants to bring about world peace" to "he wants to expel lifelong anger from his heart." This may all be true, but none of that is specific enough to become a piece of the logline. While finding true love and expelling anger are certainly valid desires, millions upon millions of characters feel those things. In fact, that's why so many back-cover blurbs sound the same. Those write-ups tend to focus on large-concept journeys such as saving the world, but neglect to share what specifically it takes to make that happen in the story. Remember, the logline is all about what makes your particular tale and character unique. So lose the broad view and figure out what is *precisely* moving your lead through his or her journey.

I have an amazing project at Fox 2000 Pictures right now, for example, with Peter Chernin as my producing partner, called *Reboot*. I could never have sold it based on describing just a general "want" for the lead character of Wren. She wants to be human. But what does that really mean?

Wren is the most famous reboot: She came back to life after being dead for an astonishing 178 minutes, which made her a bit robotic. But contrary to what you might think, what she wants is not simply to be human. That's too broad, too general a desire. What she wants is to regain the memories she had when she was alive (and not yet a reboot). She wants to relearn how to have emotions like humor, sadness, desire, and especially love, in order to overcome the unemotional world she's been living in since rebooting. Now *that's* a powerfully specific want, and it helped me set up the property as a new adaptation, a feature film project.

Here's an example of a logline that was submitted to me which needed to get rid of the generalization and focus instead on the specific:

ORIGINAL

An American woman's desire to change the world leads her to a Somalian camp where she teaches two women how to be independent and, ultimately, free.

While changing the world is an admirable goal, it doesn't work here because it is just too general a concept. Think about how many stories involve that topic; the list is endless. Therefore, it's necessary to become laser-focused on the American's *specific* goal, the thing she does which drives the story forward and also, of course, holds the most inherent drama: Always remember, you are selling, selling, selling.

In talking further with the content writer, it became clear to me that her protagonist's journey was definitely not defined by the ever-so-general "desire to change the world." In fact, the American woman's true motivation is listed in the original logline, but not until the very end—what I consider burying the lede. Her true aim in the story, as it turned out, was to *free* these Somalian women from their circumstances (horrifically bad marriages), at great risk to herself. So, keeping in mind what the protagonist really wants and being as specific as possible throughout, here's the redo:

REDO

An American risks her own life to free two highly oppressed and abused Somalian women from their prison-like marriages.

Now we understand that her pursuit of freeing the Somalian women is what is motivating her actions throughout the story, and the danger to her in doing so is clear. Her journey is very easily defined in this version, because the Somalian women's freedom is *specifically* what she wants to achieve—rather than the broad "desire to change the world." And, of course, in trying to achieve that goal, she is putting her own life at risk.

Sometimes, a writer's understanding of what his or her character wants isn't too general, it's just fixated on the wrong details. In other words, the person's desire is directed toward something that isn't actually propelling him or her through the story. Here's an example in which the protagonist's goal needs to be restructured and redefined:

ORIGINAL

A chemist with the world's most discerning nose must forgo her dream to work in the family's soybean plant.

First of all, I don't think that the writer meant that the chemist's dream was to work in the family soybean plant, but that's how it currently reads. Secondly, the bummer of having to work at the plant isn't what's driving the story forward. What kind of a dramatic journey is expressed with: "Oh, well, bummer, I have to work in my family's soybean plant?" None. So what does the chemist really want? What is her dream specifically? Again, what is moving the action along from plot point to plot point through the manuscript?

After posing these questions to the content creator, I finally learned the real story, which thankfully also included the answer to why it mattered that she had a discerning nose—she was creating a love potion. This was the dream the original piece was referring to. The tease about her having a dream was unnecessary. I needed to know *exactly* what the dream was so I could help the writer create a better logline. It's all about the specifics. Once the focus was shifted to that element, the love potion, the logline suddenly became much clearer and very different:

REDO

When a chemist's half-baked love-potion perfume is stolen, she must neutralize it before everyone in the world falls in love with someone unsuitable.

The writer never thought about what the chemist actually wanted, which was to create a working love potion. So when the character instead creates a concoction that doesn't work properly and it gets out, her journey becomes to find a way to fix that nightmare so others won't suffer the ramifications. Now that we know what the protagonist actually wants, her journey reveals itself.

It's a huge pet peeve of mine when writers send me supposed loglines like "A woman believed her fear of her past was over but she was wrong." I have no idea what exactly the woman is afraid of, and because that description sounds like a million other stories I've read, I don't much care. What the protagonist wants—to overcome her past, apparently—is so general, it doesn't entice me to want to find out more or to learn why this story is worth reading. Defining what the protagonist wants is paramount to creating a logline that will make a reader or viewer intrigued and interested in your particular story.

I remember being on the Sony lot once and bumping into a screenwriter I'd worked with in the past. He seemed a bit down so I asked what was wrong. He admitted that he felt he'd just blown an important meeting because he was asked what was motivating his lead character and he fumbled through a rambling answer. I asked him to tell me about it. His story focused on a female psychologist who was reinventing the way anger management groups were handled. She pioneered a new method for treatment that was poorly received initially, which had caused her loads of grief and stress, and ultimately caused her to almost lose her license.

When I asked what the writer believed was motivating the psychologist through her journey, he said it was her own family issues which caused her to want to rethink how things were done (which is what he had rambled on about in front of the executive). I asked him to be more specific and he said that her brother had had anger management problems that were treated improperly and affected her as a young girl. Yet again, I asked him to be even more specific. What were the issues with the brother and what exactly happened to the two of them as kids?

After much probing, here's what I came up with for a rough draft logline for the screenwriter, which he then asked to use for his next few pitches because it clearly and concisely explained what was motivating the character:

> *A psychologist, stabbed by her own brother in childhood, vows to change the way anger management is treated but risks her license with her unorthodox ways.*

It's amazing what a good logline, focusing specifically on what the protagonist wants, can do for both a story and, ultimately, a pitch.

At this point, we have defined who the protagonist is and explored motivations—what they want. But what if the character seems like they don't know what they want? What if the story is basically one on of self-discovery?

Chapter 6

What If They Don't Know What They Want?

WHEN A CONTENT CREATOR SAYS TO ME, "WHAT IF MY character doesn't know what they want—that's why they are on this adventure," I immediately suspect that it's actually the writer who doesn't know what the protagonist wants. It's absolutely imperative that the writer figure out that element before finalizing their entire story. Think about it: If you are on a journey with a character who doesn't know what they want, then why care about the voyage at all? It's certainly a recipe for slow pacing and rambling prose and not a good way to get someone to read your material.

Recently, when I spoke about deciding what a character wants, I was asked about the movie *Bridget Jones's Diary*, the 2001 film starring Renée Zellweger. An audience member expressed the opinion that Bridget is a character who doesn't know what she wants, so how do you deal with that? I disagreed with this idea. Bridget knows deep in her heart what she wants: someone to truly love her for who she is. Mark Darcy even states her secret desire when he says at one point in the film that he likes her "just as she is," and that throws her into turmoil. The reason Bridget seems to not know what she wants is because she just doesn't know how to actually get it. This is usually the case when it seems as if a character doesn't know what they want. They probably do know, they just aren't sure how to achieve it and must try a series of wrong moves to get to the right one.

In Bridget's case, her pursuit of numerous jobs, different beaux, the self-control to drink less alcohol, and the ever-elusive lighter weight on the scale are all a part of the journey she is on as she propels herself (and the story) toward her ultimate goal: to find the perfect guy who will accept her just the way she is. While these machinations can make it seem like Bridget is somewhat lost, in actuality her process of trial and error provides markers along the path to ultimately getting her what she truly wants. Here's my very rough draft logline:

A British woman humorously attempts to fix her crazy, messed-up life, hoping it will help her discover her perfect mate before she ends up a spinster.

As you can see, while Bridget may go through a process that seems like she's searching for what she wants, she's actually already pursuing her desire (to find Mr. Right), and that is what's propelling her through one mishap after another in each area of her life.

It's the same for a piece like *The Secret Life of Walter Mitty.* In James Thurber's short story, it may seem like Mitty has no idea what he wants because he imagines being a pilot, a surgeon, and even a killer. But what do all of these seemingly random occupations have in common? If you look closely, you'll find that what Mitty truly wants is to triumph, to have a certain level of success or acclaim in his fantasy life, since he is sadly unable to do so in his real one. That is why he pursues it all so vigilantly. He has one solid goal, which moves the story along through its many fantasy-based experiences.

Another example I was asked about was Morgan Spurlock's documentary *Super Size Me*, the 2004 social experiment in fast food gastronomy where Morgan attempts to subsist only on food from McDonalds for a month. It was suggested that he didn't know what he wanted when he began living off McDonald's food, and just took a wait-and-see approach to discover what would happen. I disagree with that assessment. I think Mr. Spurlock knew exactly what he wanted. He wanted to prove that eating nothing but fast food is not only dreadful for your exterior physique and internal health but can actually kill you. His desire to find out if that hypothesis was correct and his pursuit of the answer—by putting his own life at risk—proves that he not only knew what he wanted but was willing to go to any length to get it. And that is what makes the film so powerful.

In talking about what the protagonist wants, I also want to discuss a logline I created from a property with an unusual twist. I had a fantasy project in which the lead character went on an incredible journey through mystical lands filled with unicorns, fairies, et cetera, and I remember vividly that I had a very hard time coming up with the logline. My troubles emerged from the fact that I couldn't define what the protagonist really wanted. It was difficult to figure out the lead's desire since he wandered through so many trials and tribulations, and it was simply noted in the writing that he was always searching for the ever-so-general "most important." There were no other specifics. That somewhat spiritual element was as detailed as the writer got, and there was the additional, more problematic complication that the protagonist also ended up exactly where he began. I was confused because if he came full circle and finished in the exact spot where he started, what could he possibly have wanted? After all, you can't exactly want to end where you originated or you never would have set out in the first place, right?

After further exploring the material, talking with the writer, and breaking down the story, I finally realized that no matter how many stops there were along the way, this character still had to be on a journey toward something. The plot moved forward due to his decisions; it had nice pacing and some small urgency. There absolutely had to be something he wanted, even if that unnamed thing had been there all along. It turned out that that was the crux of the logline. Here's my rough draft:

> *A man on a fantastical journey searches for "the most important" and learns he had it all along, in the family he did not previously appreciate.*

What I realized from creating this unusual logline is that sometimes what the character wants is something they already possess. That is certainly a fairly uncommon occurrence, and most material doesn't fit this formula, but it's still something to note and keep in mind when trying to craft a logline.

So we've now uncovered a strong protagonist who drives the story by pursuing specifically what they want. But we're missing the critical last piece: what is at stake? What happens if the character doesn't succeed in achieving his or her desires?

Chapter 7

Defining What's at Stake

FOR ANY STORY, IT'S VITALLY IMPORTANT TO KNOW what's at stake. Sometimes, I refer to this crassly as the "why do I care?" element, not because I am trying to be mean, but because it is literally what makes us as an audience give a darn about the character's journey. It's what, at its simplest, keeps us reading or watching to find out what will happen at the end of the road. If the stakes aren't high enough, then we don't want to stay along for the ride.

Many writers confuse the action-oriented stakes with the emotional stakes. For example, I'll ask a writer what is at stake in a story, and they'll say that it's the protagonist's ability to find true love. That's what's at stake emotionally, and as per most broad sweeps, just too general for our logline purposes. What is really at stake is what happens if the character doesn't achieve his or her *specific* goal: to find the man she left at the altar ten years ago, for example. What happens if she doesn't find him? Will the protagonist feel forced to marry someone she doesn't love because she's pregnant and needs a father for her baby? Will she have to live as a spinster with 75 cats in the middle of the deepest wilderness in Alaska? I'm being a bit silly here, but these are the types of scenarios that define what is at stake for the lead character.

It's also important to know what happens if the character doesn't achieve his or her actual physical goal or desire, because the potential negative outcome is what adds to the overall story tension. When a writer is struggling to create a logline that sounds dramatic, it usually becomes clear that the reason is that what's at stake is missing from the logline. Here's an example of a logline in which, initially, there were no real stakes:

ORIGINAL

A princess must travel on a long and tiring journey to find the missing gold from her kingdom.

Why is she on this journey? What happens if she doesn't achieve her goal of finding the missing gold? These are the crucial questions that must be answered in order for us to know what's at stake for the protagonist. While, of course, it's always important to define the journey, it's even more important to express what will happen if that journey is not completed successfully. That's where the drama comes from.

After talking to the content creator at length about this story, I found out what would happen to the princess if she did not recover the gold that was taken from her kingdom. This revelation made all the difference in the world: It showed me what was at stake for her if she did not achieve her goal of finding the gold and bringing it back home. It explained the reason she went on this journey in the first place, as well. Here's the rough draft redo:

REDO
A princess must rescue her kingdom's stolen gold before she is forced to marry a rich, evil sorcerer to save her people from destitution.

Now we know what will happen if the gold is not retrieved. Additionally, this revised logline tells us what's motivating the princess' journey—what's giving it its urgency. If she does not achieve her goal then her kingdom doesn't have the funds it must have, and she'll be forced to wed a tyrant, for the greater good. Her unmarried state is what is at stake if she doesn't get the gold back in time. Notice that because we now know what will happen if she doesn't retrieve the riches, her scenario feels more pressing.

Here's another example of a logline where the stakes are missing:

ORIGINAL
A dot-com millionaire returns to his hometown to deliver the keynote speech at his old high school graduation.

My very next question to the content creator is: "So what?" Why does it matter whether or not he delivers the speech? What is at stake? What happens if he doesn't deliver it and, alternately, what happens if he does? If I don't have these answers in the logline then I don't care about the protagonist or his journey. Here's my rough draft redo after spending some time talking to the writer:

REDO

A millionaire must deliver a humble keynote speech to try to win back his first love.

This is obviously quite different, and that is because we now know the value of the speech; we know what is at stake. If he gives the speech poorly or says the wrong thing, he will never attract his true love again. Notice, by the way, that I removed all reference to the high school. That's because it doesn't matter where he delivers his speech. It only matters that the logline portrays what's needed to have the desired response of winning back the girl.

The other reason it's so imperative to define what is at stake is because, as you write, that information helps keep the story focused on what is really important. Without it, sometimes writers end up meandering through their stories without much direction—what I call an event-to-event-to-event problem. You have the scenarios in place but they lack all impact or meaning. In the earlier logline, for example, by keeping what will happen to the princess if she fails at the forefront, it's easy to make sure that every circumstance along her adventure has both exigency and the force to move her trip forward along its path. Strong, specific stakes make the reason for her journey abundantly clear.

Below is another example in which the stakes needed to be more fully defined. It's also unusual in that a question is used as a logline. I personally don't recommend using a query as your selling sentence, because a logline is always supposed to provide answers, not pose more questions. The reader obviously can't answer the question, having never read the original material, so using this method essentially falls into the category of a tease, which doesn't help you sell your work. Here's the original logline that was submitted:

ORIGINAL

A man's unique skin can set anything on fire, but is he the arsonist that's got Texas law enforcement in knots?

My first question, of course, putting into practice all we have learned so far, is if the man with the unique skin is the one on the journey, what does he want? From this logline and from speaking to the writer it seems that he does not want to be blamed for the numerous arson fires stumping the police. But that's a negative goal and rather passive: It's what he *doesn't* want. So what is more active and can fully explain what he does want? Together, we determined that we should just flip the information and craft the logline so that he actively wants to prove that he is innocent of the egregious crimes being blamed on him. The logline also has to include what is at stake—what happens if he doesn't prove his innocence—which was not mentioned in the original sentence at all. Here is the rough draft redo:

REDO

A man whose skin can start fires must prove he's innocent of serial arson or be put to death for homicides he did not commit.

The gist of the new logline is not really that different from the intent behind the original one. The redo just has everything more explained and defined so that there is no guessing required. More important, it highlights what is at stake if the lead character fails to prove his innocence.

In one of my seminars at a writers' conference, I was told about a story that was essentially about a man finding out that Lee Harvey Oswald did not kill John F. Kennedy. After hearing the very long tale, I asked the writer: "So what?"

The writer seemed perplexed. "So what?" he asked.

"Yes," I answered, "Why do I care that the protagonist found out that Oswald did not kill Kennedy?"

"What do you mean?" said the attendee.

That's when I got down to specifics. "What happens if he lets that fact be known? Will the Earth explode because history is wrong? Will he lose the love of his life because she'll think he's crazy and put him in an insane asylum? *What is at stake?*"

The writer looked at me sadly and said, "But that's it. I already wrote the whole book!"

This is the number one reason to do your logline first, during the fleshing-out process as you create your story rather than after you've written your entire work.

Now that poor guy has to go back and redo a great big portion of his writing because he didn't figure out what was at stake *first.* Now, I haven't read the full piece, obviously, but I can almost guarantee that the protagonist meanders around through one event after another with no real purpose until he stumbles upon the historically relevant information. How do I know? *Because there is nothing motivating his journey.* Afterward, I assume he wanders again, since nothing is really at stake. The writer had no concept of what happened once that important information was actually revealed.

Now that we understand the importance of defining what's at stake, I think it's essential to discuss the instances where what's at stake is already inherently defined within the logline. I appreciate when this occurs. My logline gets shorter and tighter all by itself, since I don't have to actually spell out the stakes.

Chapter 8

When What's at Stake Is Already Defined

AS MENTIONED EARLIER, SOMETIMES THE STAKES ARE already inherent in the logline without having to be explicitly spelled out, such as when the story is about a protagonist fleeing a known killer. Just the fact that the murderer has taken people's lives before makes it clear that the protagonist's life is what's at risk. This doesn't occur all that often, but when it does, creating the logline becomes much easier: You no longer have to include more words to describe what is at stake. Your sentence becomes shorter, tighter, and more focused all by itself. Here's an example of a rough draft logline in which the stakes are already inherent in the establishment of the protagonist and what she wants:

An 89-year-old nun commits to attempting completion of every item on her bucket list.

The idea that the nun has to try to achieve every item on that list *before she dies* is already implied. There is no need to spell out the fact that she has to do everything she wanted to do before her death because it's already built in to both her age and the definition of a bucket list: a list that includes the things you haven't yet done throughout your life and which you want to achieve before death takes you.

Another example in which the stakes are already implied by the rest of the logline comes from a children's property that was brought to me a few years ago. Here's the rough draft:

> *A diabetic kid is trapped inside a chocolate factory by a fiendish tooth-decay villain.*

There's no need to continue the logline by pointing out that if the kid doesn't get out he'll have to consume chocolate to survive and have a diabetic reaction that could kill him. That is already implied by the fact that the protagonist suffers from diabetes to begin with and that he's trapped in a place with nothing but sugary food to eat.

Occasionally, I come across a property where the stakes are obvious simply because of the vast divide between two characters. I call it the Romeo and Juliet logline because of the impossible rift between the Capulets and the Montagues in that famous story. Here's an example: One day, I was asked by an agent I work with to help him sell a story for one of his clients—he was struggling to find the hook. He gave me the long plot summary and asked if I could help him create a logline from it. In an early version, before I figured out what was wrong, I actually listed the stakes:

ORIGINAL

A US marshal finds the love of his life but, after a great deal of digging, unfortunately finds out that she's the daughter of NY's most powerful mafia kingpin, which puts their relationship at risk.

Of course, I knew that "relationship at risk" was much too general, but this was an early draft of the logline. Then I realized that I could actually cut that part out entirely, because the stakes were already obvious due to the Romeo and Juliet nature of the story. He is a US marshal and she's related to the mob, so the problems are inherent in any relationship they may pursue. Here's a later version, rough but nearly finished, without the spelled-out general stakes which bogged down the earlier logline:

REDO

A US marshal finds the love of his life, only to discover she's the daughter of NY's most powerful mafia kingpin.

This is not only much tighter but also focuses on what's at stake without stating it outright. In its brevity, it highlights the extremes of both marshal and mafia in the love story. What's at stake is clear: it would be virtually impossible for these two to get together without there being problems from one side or the other (and probably both).

Another good example of a Romeo and Juliet logline coming into play is the film *Pretty Woman* with Julia Roberts and Richard Gere. Here's my rough draft version:

A prostitute unfortunately falls for a client, a wealthy industrialist who doesn't believe in love.

We know what's at risk is her heart, but we don't have to add an ending such as "which makes their relationship impossible" because that's implied by each character's definition. They are at two ends of the spectrum. She's a lady of the evening, and he's a very rich gentleman with no time for matters of the heart, so the two can't end up together without there being big problems with the match.

Usually, after I create a logline, I'll look at the stated stakes and ask myself: "Do I really need this?" I try to determine if the logline works just as well without it, if the stakes are already implied somehow without me spelling them out. It's a good habit to get into. Define the stakes, always, but then revisit and see if you really need to write them out or not.

It should be crystal clear already that a logline is an indispensable tool. First of all, it helps a writer (and a reader) figure out who the protagonist really is: whose actions are driving the story forward and moving the action along. Secondly, it helps to get laser-focused on what that protagonist wants, what's motivating the journey that they are on, what's pushing them forward from one event to another. Lastly, it instills urgency and keeps the reader interested by explaining what is truly at stake, why what's happening matters, and what the consequences are if the character does not achieve the goal.

Now that we know the three main components involved, let's start to explore and understand the detailed rules for crafting the perfect logline.

Chapter 9

Only
a Sentence

WE KNOW ALL OF THE IMPORTANT MAIN ELEMENTS OF a logline, but how long should it be? Many years ago, a writing instructor told me to imagine taking five dollars out of my pocket for every word I put on the page. I found this to be invaluable advice, and I apply it constantly during logline generation and revision. It's amazing what you can cut out when it's costing you. With inflation since then, let's just say ten dollars per word.

I was just recently at ScriptDC, a Women in Film and Video conference in Washington, DC, where actors did readings of screenwriters' first four script pages out loud. During that experience, I shared this advice. The first performance was from a script with a great premise but the reading was interminable because it was excruciatingly overwritten. The actor reading the narration went on and on while the actual dialogue was minimal. When there *was* dialogue, most of it seemed repetitive. I told the writer to go back and revise with this ten-dollar rule in mind. I was convinced that what took four pages originally could actually be told in only one, perhaps less. To me, it's like having a big red pen as you read, only better, because, in theory, it affects your pocketbook so you are more apt to use the pen liberally.

Why is it important to have this frugal perspective? Because attention spans and time are both extremely short these days. No editor, agent, publisher, or executive wants to slog through a lengthy logline. No matter how long the manuscript is, it can *always* be successfully broken down into one strong, tight sentence. Here's an example I received from a content creator trying to cram the entire plot into one sentence, thinking that would be the logline:

ORIGINAL

When two prominent doctors suddenly die, they leave their daughter Christiana with nasty enemies to wage war against, a valuable piece of priceless art to find, a 100-year-old curse to deal with, and a deep dark secret regarding her real identity to discover—and as a naive sixteen-year-old, Christiana Chelsey only has a handful of homeless people to help her find out who really murdered her parents before she too is killed for the same unique painting that they were killed for.

This could be a great story and an amazing literary work but, sadly, no one would read past this supposed logline to find that out. It rambles on, so you assume the whole written work will be more of the same. It's also just plain painful: a run-on with way too much unnecessary information that's vague and general, and tells us almost nothing of import. It's what I kindly refer to as a hot mess. If we cut it down and add vocabulary to turn it into one strong sentence, we can see the difference a good logline makes. Here's the rough draft redo:

REDO

~~When two prominent doctors suddenly die, they leave their daughter Christiana with nasty enemies to wage war against, a valuable piece of priceless art to find, a 100-year-old curse to deal with, and a deep dark secret regarding her real identity to discover—and as~~ a *naive* GIRL ~~sixteen year old, Christiana Chelsey only has a handful of~~ RECRUITS THE *homeless* ~~people~~ *to help* ~~her find out~~ DISCOVER *who* ~~really~~ *murdered her parents* FOR A PIECE OF ARTWORK *before she* ~~too~~ *is killed for the same unique painting* ~~that they were killed for~~.

Here it is, clean:

A girl recruits the homeless to help discover who murdered her parents for a piece of artwork before she is killed for the same unique painting.

While it is much shorter, this version of the logline gives out the most pertinent and distinctive story information in a way that is clear and easy to follow. More important, from this version I know who the protagonist is, what she wants, and what is at stake if she doesn't succeed. Now, with this redone logline, I might actually consider reading the manuscript; with homeless folks as allies, it sounds like an interesting and different kind of journey.

Many times, writers tell me their property cannot possibly be broken down into only a sentence, that there are too many important elements, characters, and plot twists to fit it into such a tight structure. My answer is always the same: You are absolutely right—*you cannot possibly fit your entire story into only one sentence*. However, you are not being asked to do so. Instead, figure out what specifically makes your story unique. *That* is the heart and soul of your logline, *not your plot*.

One of my favorite examples has to do with a memoir about a woman who was incarcerated for dealing cocaine. The logline was very generic, as I recall, and had something to do with her getting caught with a pile of drugs. Uninspired but curious, I read all of her chapters about her life, her druggie boyfriend, and her journey through the prison system, but ultimately thought that overall it just wasn't unique. I had seen the movie *Traffic*, and this tale didn't seem all that different. The fact that she happened to be a real person with a true life story was definitely helpful, but I've read so many pieces about people who went through a similar journey that I kept asking myself my favorite question: *How can I sell this?*

I asked the content creator to take me through all the details that weren't in her pages. Slowly, the truly unique part of this story came through. Here's the final logline that I generated:

This is the true story of a girl who, at only 19, became one of the biggest drug dealers in US history.

Now, isn't that a story you want to read? And, as you can see, it's not a recitation of her complicated plot. Note, too, that what is at stake isn't spelled out here either, because it's implied by the fact that she's a drug kingpin. I'm focusing solely on the most unique parts of the tale, her young age and the huge scope of what she became involved in, in order to create a logline that would help the story be incredibly marketable.

While there is often a great deal of hemming and hawing initially about my one-sentence-only format, I find that after accepting and adopting this principle, many writers begin to get inspired by the challenge of trying to learn to focus only on what is truly unique. By cutting out bits or rephrasing to make the logline shorter, they soon find that the overall impact of the sentence comes from using fewer words and choosing more powerful vocabulary. Here's an example of small adjustments to make a logline more compelling:

ORIGINAL

A woman in love with a bad boy who is actually the devil finds out that if she makes him her husband she won't be able to be with her family ever again.

While this actually isn't bad for a first pass, look what changing the number of words, shifting their order, and adjusting the vocabulary does to the power of the logline:

REDO

A woman in love with the devil learns that if she marries him, she will lose her family forever.

The actual changes made were fairly small, but the difference to the logline was big and definitely worth it. Even though I've been writing and rewriting loglines for years, I am still always thrilled and impressed by the difference slight adjustments can make to the overall impact. You only have a single sentence for your logline, so why not make that sentence the most powerful it can possibly be, right?

I've gone to meetings that were supposed to be half an hour, but the executive was running late and suddenly it's almost lunchtime. This happened when I was going in to try to sell *Girl's Guide to Witchcraft* to ABC Family. Without warning, my pitch had to be condensed into ten minutes or suffer by being rescheduled to a later date. When this happens, as it does quite often, I usually choose to keep the appointment because (1) with the exec feeling bad about what's happened, he or she is usually in a more positive state of mind to receive and possibly buy my story and (2) with my final logline for the project firmly in my mind, I know I can literally sell it in a sentence. Whatever time I get after that is just gravy.

We know now that a logline should be only a sentence, but how can that be achieved? What should get cut out in the process of streamlining the logline?

Chapter 10

What's in a Name?

WHILE WRITING AND REWRITING THE LOGLINE, WHAT exactly can be taken out and what should be left in? These are the hardest questions, and when I look to hire screenwriters for adaptation, being able to answer these questions well is part of the skill set I require. It's important that screenwriters have the ability to know how to separate the wheat from the chaff in a novel during the process of adjusting it to become a feature film, movie of the week, or TV series. What needs to be left in so that fans of the literary material won't be disappointed? And what can be taken out because it's not visual enough for screen? There's a fine line to walk on both sides. With regard to what to cut to create a tight logline, there are, of course, rules that I've discovered through the trial and error process. But rules were also meant to be broken.

It's kind of like when you are learning to edit film. My favorite teacher at USC film school, Arnold Baker, taught us all the basics of starting with the master shot, cutting to the two-shot, then to the single and then to the opposing single shot. However, the next week he started the class by telling us to throw out all the editing knowledge we had just learned. When asked about this odd teaching method, he said that we had to solidly learn the rules first before we could begin to break them by trying something new and different. He was a smart man, and I use this method to this day. If you learn the rules first, then you know how and when it's worthwhile to break them. But how do you start?

As far as I'm concerned, the first information to cut is always the character names. Why? Because if the logline is at the top of your query letter (as it should be) or, alternately, the first thing you say to an agent or potential reader or viewer, there is no reference for who the character is yet—so the name has no meaning. Stephanie, George, Jack, Jane, and Terry don't have any value until the full story itself is read. Additionally, at ten dollars per word, why use up precious page space with something that does not help you sell? No use of proper names will ever help you to market your material. Here's an example of a logline I received for which cutting character names greatly streamlined the sentence, even in its infancy:

ORIGINAL

Life begins to unravel for a husband and wife, Andrew and Lilah Kenworth, after Andrew rediscovers an old letter he never told his wife, Lilah, about, and it threatens to reveal a betrayal toward Lilah from over twenty years ago. It turns out that Andrew hid the only correspondence her deceased fiancé, Mark Trent, sent her before he was killed, and the concealment ultimately ruins their marriage.

REDO

Life begins to unravel for a husband and wife, Andrew and Lilah Kenworth, after Andrew HE rediscovers an old letter he never told his wife, Lilah, about, and it threatens to reveal a betrayal toward Lilah from over twenty years ago. It turns out that Andrew HE hid the only correspondence her deceased fiancé, Mark Trent, sent her before he was killed, and the concealment ultimately ruins their marriage.

CLEAN

Life begins to unravel for a husband and wife after he rediscovers an old letter he never told his wife about and it threatens to reveal a betrayal from over twenty years ago—that he hid the only correspondence her deceased fiancé sent before he was killed—and the concealment ultimately ruins their marriage.

By cutting out Andrew and Lilah Kenworth's names, something wonderfully helpful is revealed. It suddenly becomes clear that the real protagonist is Andrew and not Lilah—an insight created solely by cutting the names out of the logline.

Taking out Mark Trent's name also helps tighten the sentence, because it prevents the break in pacing created by including it. Chopping out all three names helps drastically shorten the length without losing anything important, since the reader has yet to discover who these folks are. There were a few additional cuts needed before arriving at the final, solid logline, but deleting the names already helped immensely. Then I continued to distill the logline even further. Remember, at ten dollars per word it's important to streamline as much as possible in order to highlight the important elements. Here's the next redo:

REDO

~~Life begins to unravel for~~ *a husband* ~~and wife after he~~ *rediscovers* A ~~an old~~ *letter he never told his wife about* ~~and it threatens to reveal a betrayal from over twenty years ago—that he hid~~ *the only correspondence her deceased fiancé sent before he was killed—and the concealment* ~~ultimately~~ *ruins their marriage.*

CLEAN

A husband rediscovers a letter he never told his wife about, the only correspondence her deceased fiancé sent before he was killed, and the concealment ruins the marriage.

Obviously, this needs quite a bit more work, but let's review: The start was to remove all proper names. From making those edits, it became clear that the next step was to cut the wife's perspective, since the husband is the protagonist. He is the one with something to conceal, which is the element pushing the story forward, propelling him on his journey. Finally, a few additional cuts were made to tighten and focus. We'll further discuss this finessing step later.

Another reason I like to cut out proper names first is that it gives me somewhere to start. When I'm stumped on how to fix a logline, I always appreciate having the ability to at least cut it down a bit in this fashion so I feel like I've made some prog-

ress. Here's another example where chopping out names helped
a great deal:

ORIGINAL

*Miranda and her five brothers, Andrew, Kevin, Donny,
Chuck, and Steven, all lived at the parsonage until that
fateful day when their mother, Annie, died, thanks to her
lover, Sam, which forced them all to figure out new lives
for themselves.*

While there's a great deal of work to be done to the logline itself,
check out the difference simply cutting out the names makes:

REDO

~~Miranda~~ *A GIRL and her five brothers,~~Andrew, Kevin,
Donny, Chuck and Steven,~~ all lived at the parsonage
until that fateful day when their mother,~~Annie,~~ died,
thanks to her lover,~~Sam,~~ which forced them all to figure
out new lives for themselves.*

CLEAN

*A girl and her five brothers all lived at the parsonage until
that fateful day when their mother died, thanks to her lover,
which forced them all to figure out new lives for themselves.*

Of course there is much more to be done, but just cutting
out proper names gives us a much better base to work from. If
nothing else, it's a fresh way to start. I then tightened this logline
a bit more and made it more active.

REDO

A girl and her five brothers are kicked out of the parsonage when their mother dies, forcing them into a harsh life on the streets.

Then I had to call the writer to find out further details of her story (which was still being written) so that I could replace "harsh life on the streets." That is, of course, too general. Only then could I continue through the process.

REDO

A girl and her brothers are kicked out of the parsonage when their mother dies, forcing them into prostitution and pickpocketing to survive.

Note that I also removed "five," because at this point, we really don't care how many brothers she has, only that she has them.

REDO

A girl is evicted from her safe parsonage to the hell of prostitution and pickpocketing for survival.

You can see that I ultimately removed all reference to their mother dying: For the logline, it's only important that they got evicted from the parsonage (because of its complete opposition to life on the streets), not why they got kicked out. I also removed her brothers, because the girl is actually the sole protagonist. While these unfortunate events happened to everyone in the family, it is her journey that is keeping the story in motion. I also decided not to specifically state what is at stake, because this is a case in which the risk is inherent in the circumstances; if she's prostituting and pickpocketing to survive, then her life is what is at stake if she isn't successful at those things. I went through quite a few extensively rewritten drafts of this particular logline, but what got me going at the very start was removing all the proper names so I'd have a decent foundation to work from.

As you might imagine, the exception to this rule is any instance where the name is integral to the story itself, like Queen Elizabeth or Adolf Hitler. Usually these exceptions come from memoirs and/or true stories, but they can also be intrinsic to fiction: Superman, for example. You could certainly start your logline with something like "A man with super-human abilities . . ." instead, but that's quite a lot of words (at ten dollars per word) when just "Superman" will do. More important, however, the character of Superman is already highly recognizable, and therefore helps the story to stand out in a crowded marketplace. It also indicates a built-in audience—two big pluses in marketing your material to the masses.

Cutting out names is step number one to cutting down your sentence into something focused and tight, but that's only a beginning. Here are a few logline samples you can try, to practice this skill. After you've mastered them, we'll move on to the next step in streamlining your logline.

Chapter 10
Sample Loglines

1. When Amanda secretly reveals to her boyfriend Josh that she's a lesbian, he tells his brother Charles and the entire school, causing her best friends, Charity and Jessica, to help her get revenge by making him appear naked at graduation.

2. In 1943, Oliver begs his sister Diane for an intro to her hot best friend and his crush, Jean-Jean, but his pals Eddie and Irwin tell him that if he dates Jean-Jean, who's an African American girl, his chances of becoming a draft pick will be ruined.

3. Asia Harlin and her friends Gigi, Iliana, and Tammy take the drugs Meryl Sanchez provides to keep thin for modeling, but when she is diagnosed by Dr. Moore with body dysmorphia, it's a life-and-death struggle to get back to looking "normal."

4. Antonia Snow, a librarian, receives a children's book collection from an unknown Aunt Eleanor and discovers there's magic inside the volumes which must be

protected or Cinderella, Glinda the Good Witch, Hansel and Gretel, and all the other "imaginary characters" will die.

5. Tikka the Toucan and her zoo buddies, Martin the Monkey, Ferdinand the Frog, and Egrid the Elephant are accidentally swapped with animals destined for a wilderness camp and must find a way back to their safe enclosures before Mr. Kretch, their trainer, discovers they are missing.

Answers to
Chapter 10 Samples

1.

ORIGINAL

When Amanda secretly reveals to her boyfriend Josh that she's a lesbian, he tells his brother Charles and the entire school, causing her best friends, Charity and Jessica, to help her get revenge by making him appear naked at graduation.

REDO

When ~~Amanda~~ A GIRL secretly reveals to her boyfriend ~~Josh~~ that she's a lesbian, he tells ~~his brother Charles and~~ the entire school, causing her best friends~~, Charity and Jessica,~~ to help her get revenge by making him appear naked at graduation.

CLEAN

When a girl secretly reveals to her boyfriend that she's a lesbian, he tells the entire school, causing her best friends to help her get revenge by making him appear naked at graduation.

2.

ORIGINAL

In 1943, Oliver begs his sister Diane for an intro to her hot best friend and his crush, Jean-Jean, but his pals Eddie and Irwin tell him that if he dates Jean-Jean, who's an African American girl, his chances of becoming a draft pick will be ruined.

REDO

In 1943, ~~Oliver~~ A WHITE FOOTBALL STAR begs his sister ~~Diane~~ for an intro to her hot best friend ~~and his crush, Jean-Jean,~~ but his pals ~~Eddie and Irwin~~ tell him that if he dates ~~Jean-Jean who's~~ an African American girl, his chances of becoming a draft pick will be ruined.

CLEAN

In 1943, a white football star begs his sister for an intro to her hot best friend, but his pals tell him that if he dates an African American girl, his chances of becoming a draft pick will be ruined.

3.

ORIGINAL

Asia Harlin and her friends Gigi, Iliana, and Tammy take the drugs Meryl Sanchez provides to keep thin for modeling, but when she is diagnosed by Dr. Moore with body dysmorphia, it's a life-and-death struggle to get back to looking "normal."

REDO

~~Asia Harlin~~ A GIRL and her friends ~~Gigi, Iliana, and Tammy~~ take ~~the~~ drugs ~~Meryl Sanchez provides~~ to keep thin for modeling, but when she is diagnosed ~~by Dr. Moore~~ with body dysmorphia, it's a life-and-death struggle to get back to looking "normal."

CLEAN

A girl and her friends take drugs to keep thin for modeling, but when she is diagnosed with body dysmorphia, it's a life-and-death struggle to get back to looking "normal."

4.

ORIGINAL

Antonia Snow, a librarian, receives a children's book collection from an unknown Aunt Eleanor and discovers there's magic inside the volumes which must be protected or Cinderella, Glinda the Good Witch, Hansel and Gretel, and all the other "imaginary characters" will die.

REDO

~~Antonia Snow,~~ a librarian, receives a children's book collection ~~from an unknown Aunt Eleanor~~ and discovers there's magic inside the volumes which must be protected or ~~Cinderella, Glinda the Good Witch, Hansel & Gretel~~ ~~and~~ all the ~~other~~ "imaginary characters" will die.

CLEAN

A librarian receives a children's book collection and discovers there's magic inside the volumes which must be protected or all the "imaginary characters" will die.

5.

ORIGINAL

Tikka the Toucan and her zoo buddies, Martin the Monkey, Ferdinand the Frog, and Egrid the Elephant are accidentally swapped with animals destined for a wilderness camp and must find a way back to their safe enclosures before Mr. Kretch, their trainer, discovers they are missing.

REDO

~~Tikka the~~ A Toucan and her zoo buddies, ~~Martin the Monkey, Ferdinand the Frog and Egrid the Elephant,~~ are accidentally swapped with animals destined for a wilderness camp and must find a way back to their safe enclosures before ~~Mr. Kretch,~~ their trainer, discovers they are missing.

CLEAN

A toucan and her zoo buddies are accidentally swapped with animals destined for a wilderness camp and must find a way back to their safe enclosures before their trainer discovers they are missing.

Chapter 11

Ageism

AFTER YOU ELIMINATE NAMES IN YOUR LOGLINE, THE second thing that's important to cut is any reference to the age of the character or characters. Why? Because this could hurt your ability to entice potential readers. For example, if someone is disinterested in reading about thirteen-year-olds, when that's listed as the age of the character in your logline they won't read any further. But if you say "a very young boy," you may still get them to read the rest of your query letter and perhaps even the manuscript. Why give them a reason to pass if you don't have to?

Before I go into any pitch with a company, I make a list of reasons why they might say no. Then I try to find ways to tackle those elements ahead of time, so by the time they hear the pitch, I've already removed the easy ways for them to pass on the project. Case in point: I had a project I wanted to set up with Ridley Scott's company, Scott Free. Having met with their executive in the past, I knew they weren't looking for any YA (young adult) material. However, I had a YA property that fit their wish list in every other way—it was sci-fi, it was grounded, it had a male lead, and it was filled with action and intrigue. So, before I sent them my logline, I removed any reference to the age of the protagonist—who was actually sixteen—and they loved the story. Subsequently, of course, I let them know that the original material had been young adult, but I then asked the author (since the book was still being written) to change the protagonist into his twenties at the request of the executive. The beauty is that the change in age didn't affect the story at all, because the age wasn't truly important to what was happening. Just think, this project would have never gotten past the initial query had the logline indicated that the lead was only sixteen.

Here is good example of a logline that is helped out a great deal by taking out the names and age factors:

ORIGINAL

Jacki Stavros, a 15-year-old rebel teen, decides to steer her band to the heights of New York's punk scene at a very early age, without ever compromising, but with snark comes problems, and the teenager ends up bottoming out from drugs and alcohol.

REDO

~~Jacki Stavros,~~ a ~~15-year-old~~ rebel ~~teen, decides~~ FIGHTS to steer her band to the heights of New York's punk scene ~~at a very early age, without ever compromising,~~ but ~~with snark comes problems, and the teenager~~ ends up bottoming out from drugs and alcohol.

CLEAN

A rebel fights to steer her band to the heights of New York's punk scene but ends up bottoming out from drugs and alcohol.

The name, of course, was cut immediately. Then the age was chopped out, along with the note that she's a teen, because that isn't important for the logline. It's not vital to this particular story. More important, this version can now appeal to a broader audience. Hearing that she fought to steer her band to the top at a very early age isn't essential either, because the emphasis should be on her action, not the age at which she did it. The only way I might have left in the age would have been if this had taken place in a high school, because then her being fifteen would mean something to the piece. While the logline still needs quite a bit of work, you can see that just starting out by cutting the basics of name and age help immensely in terms of length, impact, and focus.

Here's another example I worked on with a writer, in which I immediately cut out the ages of the characters:

ORIGINAL

A 40-year-old lonely gynecologist, Frederick, becomes insanely obsessed with Carolyn, his 30-year-old, already-married female patient, and stalks her until receiving counseling, from her husband.

Remember, the start is removing the names and the next step is to remove the characters' ages. Always remind yourself of the ten dollars per word rule as well.

REDO

A ~~40-year-old lonely~~ gynecologist~~, Frederick,~~ becomes insanely obsessed with ~~Carolyn,~~ his ~~30-year-old,~~ already-married ~~female~~ patient and stalks her until receiving counseling, from her husband.

CLEAN

A gynecologist becomes insanely obsessed with his already-married patient and stalks her until receiving counseling, from her husband.

I'd still rework this logline quite a bit more, but cutting out the ages (and, of course, the names) has given us a great base to work from.

As usual, there are exceptions to the rule, such as when the age is vital to the plot—à la *The Curious Case of Benjamin Button*—but these are few and far between. In fact, I rarely end up keeping the age of any character in a logline. Recently, at a conference, a writer expounded upon the fact that her story would appeal to an underserved audience of those over 50 because her lead was 60 years old. I told her that by saying that, she's not accomplishing what she wants—to sell her story—because Hollywood sadly focuses on 18- to 35-year-old viewers and will simply pass on what they'd consider a "senior" story. I told her instead to explain why her story would appeal to an audience of all ages, because it touches on both the underserved older population as well as the much younger and more desirable demographics.

Another example of a situation in which you want to keep in

age markers is when that is the crux of the story. For example, I have a project with the Gotham Group right now based on a cool novel Karen Dionne is working on, which involves some kids trying to find out why everyone 17 and older is suddenly dying. Our lead character is a 16-year-old girl who is nearing her next birthday. Of course, in this instance, I would actually emphasize her age in the logline, because that's the ticking clock that motivates her journey and gives it terrific urgency. She will literally die on her seventeenth birthday if she (and the others) don't figure out what's going on. Here's the logline:

A 16-year-old girl must discover what's killing everyone 17 and older before she dies on her next birthday.

As you can see, this is a definite exception to the age-cutting rule.

Right now I'm considering taking on a cool science fiction story that I was sent, a barely finished young adult manuscript. While I love its main concept of an elimination squad, I'm just not sure if I can sell it in the current marketplace. After *Twilight, Hunger Games, Divergent,* and even my own project with Peter Chernin at Fox 2000 (which I mentioned earlier in this book), *Reboot,* the YA arena in feature films is extremely saturated. In order to make this story move, I've decided to speak with the writer's agent and ask if I can adjust it for any age, rather than YA. If the lead character and her love interest are in their twenties, for example, I don't feel it will adversely affect the story and it may give me an extra boost in being able to set it up for adaptation. If the agent agrees, my logline will have no mention of high school, teens, or young adults at all, no matter what the manuscript actually contains. If I can get the writer to consider changing the ages in the original material, since it's still in process, so much the better. Here's a rough draft of what my logline will probably look like:

> *A soldier in a special Elimination Unit is captured by an outlaw who shows her evidence against the government, and she must decide to either uphold Command or fight alongside the fugitives.*

Even in this rough form, the logline can show how the potential film might well appeal to a broad audience, and thus be infinitely more marketable than if it was positioned in that "teenage story" box.

Now we know names and ages can be cut, and that's a great start, but it's not enough. Here are a few sample loglines to help you practice what's been explored so far, then we'll discover what else can be removed to make the logline better, tighter, more sellable.

Chapter 11
Sample Loglines

---

1. A 17-year-old teen rebels against his parents, Donna and Henry, until they throw him out and he has to learn to survive on the mean streets of Los Angeles with Sandy, another young runaway, as his jaded guide.

2. Nurse Nancy Clemens has been accused of the elder abuse of her 76-year old patient and must fight the system and her boss of 18 years, Donald Mason, in order to retain her job and clear her name.

3. In the year 2247, space travel is commonplace and Selsi, a 15-year-old light source mechanic, keeps the sky-movers running smoothly until she discovers her nemesis, 17-year-old Waven, has hidden a deadly gas in the vehicles of High Chief Resa and the other prominent citizens of their colony.

4. Kelvin Hooper, an 18-year-old wannabe geneticist, finds out that 7-year-old Angel has a special gift—she no longer gets any older—but when Kelvin tries to discover the source of Angel's immortality, Kelvin inadvertently triggers rapid aging and must reverse what he and his best friend, Olive, have done before Angel dies.

5. Deana and Joshua are two 40-somethings whose marriage has become stale, so they both begin to secretly pursue flings with their young 20-something next-door neighbors, Stacey and Andrew, until Deana and Josh finally learn to appreciate what they have in each other.

Answers to Chapter 11 Samples

1.

ORIGINAL

A 17-year-old teen rebels against his parents, Donna and Henry, until they throw him out and he has to learn to survive on the mean streets of Los Angeles with Sandy, another young runaway, as his jaded guide.

REDO

A ~~17-year-old teen~~ KID rebels against his parents, ~~Donna and Henry,~~ until they throw him out and he has to learn to survive on the mean streets of Los Angeles with ~~Sandy,~~ another ~~young~~ runaway, as his jaded guide.

CLEAN

A kid rebels against his parents until they throw him out and he has to learn to survive on the mean streets of Los Angeles with another runaway as his jaded guide.

2.

ORIGINAL

Nurse Nancy Clemens has been accused of the elder abuse of her 76-year-old patient and must fight the system and her boss of 18 years, Donald Mason, in order to retain her job and clear her name.

REDO

A Nurse ~~Nancy Clemens has been~~ accused of ~~the elder~~ abuseING ~~of~~ her ~~76-year-old~~ patient ~~and~~ must fight the system and her boss ~~of 18 years, Donald Mason,~~ in order to retain her job and clear her name.

CLEAN

A nurse accused of abusing her patient must fight the system and her boss in order to retain her job and clear her name.

3.

ORIGINAL

In the year 2247, space travel is commonplace and Selsi, a 15-year-old light source mechanic, keeps the sky-movers running smoothly until she discovers her nemesis, 17-year-old Waven, has hidden a deadly gas in the vehicles of High Chief Resa and the other prominent citizens of their colony.

REDO

In the year 2247, space travel is commonplace and ~~Selsi, a 15-year-old~~ A light source mechanic~~,~~ keeps the sky-movers running smoothly until she discovers her nemesis~~,~~ ~~17-year-old Waven,~~ has hidden a deadly gas in the vehicles of ~~High Chief Resa and~~ the ~~other~~ prominent citizens of their colony.

CLEAN

In the year 2247, space travel is commonplace and a light source mechanic keeps the sky-movers running smoothly until she discovers her nemesis has hidden a deadly gas in the vehicles of the prominent citizens of their colony.

4.

ORIGINAL

Kelvin Hooper, an 18-year-old wannabe geneticist, finds out that 7-year-old Angel has a special gift—she no longer gets any older—but when Kelvin tries to discover the source of Angel's immortality, Kelvin inadvertently triggers rapid aging and must reverse what he and his best friend, Olive, have done before Angel dies.

REDO

~~Kelvin Hooper, an 18-year-old~~ A wannabe geneticist~~,~~ finds ~~out that~~ A GIRL WHO ~~7-year-old Angel has a special gift—she~~ no longer gets ~~any~~ older—but when ~~Kelvin~~ HE tries to discover the source of ~~Angel's~~ THE immortality, ~~Kelvin~~ HE inadvertently triggers rapid aging and must reverse what'S ~~he and his best friend, Olive, have~~ BEEN done before ~~Angel~~ SHE dies.

CLEAN

A wannabe geneticist finds a girl who no longer gets older but when he tries to discover the source of the immortality, he inadvertently triggers rapid aging and must reverse what's been done before she dies.

5.

ORIGINAL

Deana and Joshua are two 40-somethings whose marriage has become stale, so they both begin to secretly pursue flings with their young 20-something next-door neighbors, Stacey and Andrew, until Deana and Josh finally learn to appreciate what they have in each other.

REDO

~~Deana and Joshua are two 40-somethings~~ A COUPLE whose marriage has become stale~~, so they both begin to~~ secretly pursue flings with their ~~young 20-something next-door~~ neighbors~~, Stacey and Andrew,~~ until ~~Deana and Josh~~ finally learnING to appreciate what they have in each other.

CLEAN

A couple whose marriage has become stale secretly pursue flings with their neighbors until finally learning to appreciate what they have in each other.

Chapter 12

The Adjective Objective

THERE ARE MANY CUTS THAT NEED TO BE MADE throughout the editing process. The toughest of all, however, involves removing adjectives. They usually take up room without giving much in return, since they don't help sell a project. Many writers fall in love with their descriptive words and find it difficult to take them out. What I always tell them is that unless it helps market your story it's not worth keeping in, and it's also important to trust that the real creative writing is in the full manuscript. The logline is the way to get people to read it—so don't sabotage yourself by bogging the logline down with unnecessary adjectives.

Many content creators feel that the use of descriptive language helps show off their abilities as writers. They think that the creative adjectives they've chosen are what make them stand out and exemplify what they can do on the page. My answer is that in only one sentence not much is going to be said about your writing ability unless it's that you are able to convey the important elements of your story—who is the protagonist, what that person wants, and what is at stake—in a powerful, tight logline that also highlights what's unique about your particular tale. That is what is truly impressive.

Now that I've told you to "kill your babies," as they say in editing, here's a strong example of the judicious cutting of adjectives, which helps the logline flow:

ORIGINAL

A promiscuous and adventuresome divorcée finds herself falling deeply in love with a self-centered, obnoxious, and altogether inappropriate man, and in attempting to remove herself from his unbelievably powerful and seductive spell, she ends up hooking up with a wallflower-like, shy, and reserved woman—and surprises herself to realize she's a lesbian.

REDO

A ~~promiscuous and adventuresome~~ divorcée finds herself falling ~~deeply~~ in love with aN ~~self-centered, obnoxious, and altogether~~ inappropriate man, and in attempting to remove herself from his ~~unbelievably powerful and seductive~~ spell, she ends up hooking up with a ~~wallflower-like, shy, and reserved woman—and surprises herself to realize she's a~~ lesbian.

CLEAN

A divorcée finds herself falling in love with an inappropriate man, and in attempting to remove herself from his spell, she ends up hooking up with a lesbian.

As you can see, just removing all of the unnecessary description has made a huge difference to the logline in only one quick and easy step!

Here's another example where too many adjectives are dragging down the logline unnecessarily:

ORIGINAL

Adina, a very young girl, and her kind and generous mother must find their way out of a mysterious town with a unique element that revolves around a warlock's quirky sweetshop and a very deadly secret, which the town carefully guards—anyone who partakes of the candies can never leave.

REDO

~~Adina,~~ a ~~very young~~ girl, and her ~~kind and generous~~ mother must find their way out of a ~~mysterious~~ town with ~~a unique element that revolves around~~ a warlock's ~~quirky~~ sweetshop ~~and a very deadly secret,~~ WHERE ~~which the town carefully guards=~~anyone who partakes of the candies can never leave.

CLEAN

A girl and her mother must find their way out of a town with a warlock's sweetshop, where anyone who partakes of the candies can never leave.

The names are obviously the first thing to cut. The age-based words "very young" are unnecessary, because they don't add anything and, as mentioned, can turn off a reader who is not interested in hearing about very young protagonists. The adjectives "kind" and "generous" are also superfluous: They are bland, and don't add to the drama or stakes or action. The fact that the town is "mysterious" has nothing to do with the need to flee from it, so that too can be cut. "Quirky" is removed because we'll find out about that when we read the original work, so it's unnecessary for the logline. And lastly, "deadly" is confusing because the hook is that they can't leave, not that they'll be killed, so that was taken out as well.

As I've mentioned earlier, there are exceptions to every rule, and those exceptions actually tell you what to leave in. For example, if the adjective helps show how unique the story or concept is, then it's worth keeping. So the words "warlock's sweetshop" were left in intentionally because they are what make the story unique: This is not just any sweetshop, it's one owned by a warlock.

Here's another example of a good logline in which adjectives makes it stronger, from a property I brought to Johnny Depp's company:

A woman's idyllic homecoming is shattered when she becomes the target of a demonic coven determined to either make her a member or kill her.

Why leave in the words "idyllic" and "demonic"? Because in this particular situation, it emphasizes the extremity of the character arc. Instead of the woman going from simply a homecoming to a coven, the journey becomes more extreme when she goes from an "idyllic" homecoming to a "demonic" coven—and so the stakes are raised.

Another exception comes into play when the very description is what makes the story unique. For example, I have a project with Film Engine that's somewhat in the vein of *Die Hard*. And while I love the property, I can't sell a *Die Hard*-type project without sounding exactly like the other million action films being pitched on a daily basis. So how can I make this stand out in a crowded marketplace? As always, I need to focus on the element that makes it unique, which in this case turns out to be the character description. The protagonist is a biological warfare expert, the best in the world, in fact, but he's also something else . . . superstitious beyond belief. The guy carries around juju beads, a Saint Christopher's medal, and a multitude of other supposedly life-saving paraphernalia with him. So the logline absolutely had to convey this aspect of this unusual action hero. Those adjectives are what make him special, and therefore create a significant selling tool for the project. Here's one of the later versions of the logline:

> *A highly superstitious, world-renowned biological warfare expert must save the president's life armed only with smarts and a four-leaf clover.*

Normally, the first thing cut would be "highly superstitious," but because it is the crux of what makes this project different, I left it in and even emphasized it with the "four-leaf clover" reference. Now, at the very least, it doesn't sound like *Die Hard*, and you can see how in this particular instance the descriptive words are absolutely necessary.

Keep in mind, however, that usually adjectives are some of the first words to get cut out of a logline. At ten dollars per word, if they aren't helping you sell your story, you can't afford to keep them in your sentence.

All right, so you've learned to cut proper names, ages and age indicators, and unnecessary descriptive adjectives. What is the next step in making the logline better? We'll explore that answer after you try out a few sample loglines, applying all you have learned thus far.

Chapter 12
Sample Loglines

---

1. Thirty-two-year-old packrat and hoarder Marti meets 27-year-old clean-cut minimalist Stan and it's true love at first sight, and a quick but lovely and poignant marriage ceremony, until the two opposites realize their individual lifestyles are completely and utterly incompatible and must find a safe middle ground before a nasty divorce is their only option.

2. Four 80-year-old crusty and worn-out cowboys find themselves on an unexpectedly special journey to rescue a kidnapped little 10-year-old girl named Amy before a corrupt and evil despot remorselessly kills her.

3. In the Deep South, tensions run high when Elias Castor, a nasty, rich plantation owner, is the first to enslave a kindly white man named Jared, whom he erroneously assumes made shocking and improper advances toward his pampered young daughter, Meribelle, and the rest of Castor's black slaves rebel at Jared's treatment and ultimately kill their master, burning his house to the ground.

4. Rufus, an affectionate and spunky old junkyard dog, dies, but in heaven he is given a unique second chance to come back down to Earth with the enormous task of trying to help a solemn and silent 11-year-old boy smile again after the sad death of his beloved mother.

5. A sudden deadly winter storm traps Caroline, a new young mother, and her sickly baby Clara in the mountains, and only a crotchety old miner named Dylan and his faithful mangy mutt, Dirt, can help the two of them survive the extremely grueling conditions and help them get safely back to town by Christmas.

Answers to
Chapter 12 Samples

1.

ORIGINAL

Thirty-two-year-old packrat and hoarder Marti meets 27-year-old clean-cut minimalist Stan and it's true love at first sight, and a quick but lovely and poignant marriage ceremony, until the two opposites realize their individual lifestyles are completely and utterly incompatible and must find a safe middle ground before a nasty divorce is their only option.

REDO

~~Thirty-two-year-old packrat and~~ A hoarder ~~Marti~~ meets ~~27-year-old clean-cut~~ A minimalist ~~Stan~~ and it's true love ~~at first sight,~~ and a quick ~~but lovely and poignant~~ marriage ceremony, until theY ~~two opposites~~ realize their ~~individual~~ lifestyles are ~~completely and utterly~~ incompatible and must find ~~a safe~~ middle ground before ~~a nasty~~ divorce is their only option.

CLEAN

A hoarder meets a minimalist and it's true love and a quick marriage ceremony, until they realize their lifestyles are incompatible and must find middle ground before divorce is their only option.

2.

ORIGINAL

Four 80-year-old crusty and worn-out cowboys find themselves on an unexpectedly special journey to rescue a kidnapped little 10-year-old girl named Amy before a corrupt and evil despot remorselessly kills her.

REDO

Four ~~80-year-old~~ crusty ~~and worn-out~~ cowboys ~~find themselves on an unexpectedly special journey to~~ MUST rescue a kidnapped ~~little 10-year-old~~ girl ~~named Amy~~ before a ~~corrupt and evil~~ despot ~~remorselessly~~ kills her.

CLEAN

Four crusty cowboys must rescue a kidnapped girl before a despot kills her.

3.

ORIGINAL

In the Deep South, tensions run high when Elias Castor, a nasty, rich plantation owner, is the first to enslave a kindly white man named Jared, whom he erroneously assumes made shocking and improper advances toward his pampered young daughter, Meribelle, and the rest of Castor's black slaves rebel at Jared's treatment and ultimately kill their master, burning his house to the ground.

REDO

~~In the Deep South, tensions run high when Elias Castor,~~ ~~a nasty, rich~~ A plantation owner~~, is the first to~~ enslaves a ~~kindly~~ white man ~~named Jared,~~ whom he erroneously assumes made ~~shocking and improper~~ advances toward his ~~pampered young~~ daughter~~, Meribelle,~~ and the ~~rest~~ ~~of Castor's~~ black slaves rebel at ~~Jared's~~ THE WHITE MAN'S treatment and ultimately kill their master~~, burning his house to the ground.~~

CLEAN

A plantation owner enslaves a white man whom he erroneously assumes made advances toward his daughter, and the black slaves rebel at the white man's treatment and ultimately kill their master.

4.

ORIGINAL

Rufus, an affectionate and spunky old junkyard dog, dies, but in heaven he is given a unique second chance to come back down to Earth with the enormous task of trying to help a solemn and silent 11-year-old boy smile again after the sad death of his beloved mother.

REDO

~~Rufus, an affectionate and spunky old~~ A junkyard dog~~,~~ dies~~,~~ but ~~in heaven he~~ is given a ~~unique second~~ chance to come back ~~down to Earth with the enormous task of trying~~ to help a ~~solemn and silent 11-year-old~~ boy smile again after the ~~sad~~ death of his ~~beloved~~ mother.

CLEAN

A junkyard dog dies but is given a chance to come back to help a boy smile again after the death of his mother.

5.

ORIGINAL

A sudden deadly winter storm traps Caroline, a new young mother, and her sickly baby Clara in the mountains, and only a crotchety old miner named Dylan and his faithful mangy mutt, Dirt, can help the two of them survive the extremely grueling conditions and help them get safely back to town by Christmas.

REDO

A ~~sudden deadly winter~~ storm traps ~~Caroline,~~ a ~~new young~~ mother~~,~~ and her ~~sickly~~ baby ~~Clara~~ in the mountains, and only a crotchety ~~old~~ miner ~~named Dylan~~ and his ~~faithful mangy~~ mutt~~, Dirt,~~ can help ~~the two of~~ them survive ~~the extremely grueling conditions~~ and ~~help them~~ get safely back to town by Christmas.

CLEAN

A storm traps a mother and her baby in the mountains, and only a crotchety miner and his mutt can help them survive and get safely back to town by Christmas.

Chapter 13

Be
Specific

MANY WRITERS, ESPECIALLY THOSE WHO THINK THE logline is their back-cover blurb, end up using big general concepts in their pitch. For example, they write that their work is about "a woman on a journey toward love." The problem with using big emotional lines like this is that they make your material sound like every other book in that same genre. That's why the back-cover blurbs tend to all sound the same when browsing in a particular genre section at a bookstore. By sticking with the general, once again you are using words that don't help sell your particular story. Specifics are what highlight the elements that make your work stand out and feel different and special.

In the previous example, let's change elements of the logline to be much more specific, so the story is instead about "a woman giving her heart to a man who's in prison." Do you see how much more distinctive that sounds? A logline should always emphasize what is unique about your particular story—and the only way to do that is by being *specific*.

Here's a great example of a logline that got better and more sellable, the more specific it became. This was my initial pass at creating a logline for the story, which I eventually set up at the Disney Channel:

ORIGINAL

A girl on the fringes of the social order at her high school fights those higher up on the societal ladder, who would keep her down.

What I didn't like about this, even as a starting point, is that it reminded me too much of *Mean Girls*, and the reason it felt like that was because I was being too general about the girl's journey and how she achieved it. I also had to remind myself that the goal is always to emphasize what is unique: What was it specifically about the story that felt new and fresh and had attracted me to it? During the process of rereading the novel, I realized that I loved a sub-character, a curmudgeonly history teacher who lectures on revolution but, more importantly, inspires the lead character's journey. Suddenly, that unique aspect of the material beautifully became the focus of and force for the logline.

REDO

A girl uses the principles of revolution to change the social order at her high school and try to propel herself out of the dreaded "general population."

Concentrating on the unusual idea of using the principles of revolution to overthrow the queen bee of the school was what gave this logline its best chance at selling the material. We still reworked it a few times afterward, to raise the stakes and enhance some vocabulary, but this is a great example of how focusing on specifics while creating a logline can help emphasize the elements that have the most marketability in a story. Additionally, it helped me set up the project for adaptation, which I am absolutely sure would not have happened with the earlier iteration.

The general ideas of "finding true love," "saving the world," and "coming of age" work only to give a sense of where on the bookshelf certain material should be placed in a bookstore: in the romance, drama, or young adult section. But for our purposes, they are essentially useless, because they act in complete opposition to finding what is special about a story. Those conventional concepts are what I call "deal-killers," because they make the plot sound like many others already out there. If I took a poll of people on the street, most would say they've read or seen literally hundreds of stories in the three aforementioned arenas. So the only way to market your story is to push the idea of something *new* in those genres. It's the same in any type of selling: The most recent, hottest flavor of the month is always something touted as a thing you've never seen before. Selling a story is no different, and the only way to make it fresh is to zoom in on the specifics of the tale. Here's another example:

ORIGINAL

A boy travels the globe, changing many lives along the way.

I think I could name quite a few projects that fit into this mold of "person on an emotional journey," so this supposed logline needs a major wake-up call. I grilled the writer about what *specifics* he could tell me about what happened on the path, how *precisely* lives were changed. I also asked why this particular boy needed this adventure and why this trip was important to take right now. Here are the surprising answers in the redone logline:

REDO

A cancer-riddled boy spends his last days travelling the globe with Kickstarter funds, giving destitute families a new beginning.

Quite different, right? And infinitely more compelling because now the story sounds intriguing and I know what's *specifically* at stake, since death from cancer (indicated by "cancer-riddled" and "his last days") is involved. Now I care about what happens to this boy and I care about the journey he is on, which I did not when it was about amorphous travel and helping faceless folks for no particular reason.

In my industry, the one thing I always ask myself before sharing a logline is whether or not that sentence makes the piece sound fresh and different, because that's the only way I'm going to be able to set it up. So I'm always taken aback when writers cling to their idea of teasing the reader, of not giving away their surprise by sharing specifics. To my mind, the real surprise is that they are hiding their greatest selling tool: the elements that make their particular story unlike everyone else's in the marketplace.

Being specific also helps with trends. For example, from time to time I'll hear that a studio is looking for Christmas fare. That's great knowledge to have but, unfortunately, there's a great deal of

Christmas material in the marketplace, so this is a yearly trend in which it's very hard to stand out. Most every holiday tale has Santa or elves or reindeer or the like. In these cases, therefore, more than ever, being specific so the story feels new is incredibly important, or that project will just end up in the huge pile of holiday properties brought in to the studio because of their request.

One time, I brought Universal a new Santa Claus tale, but I knew I couldn't sell it like that or I'd just hear that they had too many new Santa stories coming in. Instead, I gave them this logline:

A husband and wife are near divorce and, since the couple is Mr. and Mrs. Claus, it's up to the elves to get them together by Dec 25th or there'll be no Christmas.

I knew the studio would get hundreds of submissions about Santa and Christmas and elves, so instead I put the emphasis on the more personal story of a couple near divorce. To me, that felt like a fresh approach. How many Christmas tales include divorce? Probably not that many. But I also changed the focus, because human relationships are what will bring in the audience: These relationships are universally relatable. Additionally, I put what was at stake first and *then* revealed that the couple was Mr. and Mrs. Claus to surprise the reader (the executive) and make the story more intriguing. This very specific logline essentially helped me let the exec know that (1) this Christmas material was different and (2) that it would appeal to a wide audience—two terrific selling tools.

Here are a few instances of too-general loglines and then their more specific first rough draft revisions. Nothing here is final, but these examples will further demonstrate the power of the specific in loglines.

ORIGINAL

True love blossoms between a newspaperman and a Western woman until her secret obsession threatens to pull them apart.

REDO

A newspaperman falls for a female miner but her insane obsession with gold forces him to ultimately abandon her in the wilderness.

ORIGINAL

During the recession, a computer-code writer is forced to take a job at a vegetarian co-op, where he learns the value of the organic rather than the synthetic.

REDO

An unemployed computer-code writer is forced to take a job at a vegetarian co-op, and discovers that super-food can do more for the brain than his expensive new mind-mastery program.

ORIGINAL

A stay-at-home mom struggles to keep her family from knowing about her past when it comes back to haunt her and threatens to drag her back into her old job.

REDO

A stay-at-home mom successfully hides that she was once a spy, until a vengeful ex-associate forces her to return to the job when he threatens her new family.

ORIGINAL

A vagrant must keep a magical bird safe at all costs because its song can do amazing things, causing others to try to steal it for their own purposes.

REDO

A vagrant's magic nightingale's song gives eternal youth, so he must keep the bird from being stolen by a king bent on immortality.

As you can see, being specific supplies the details that tell you what is special and different about the story, which provides exactly what you need to sell it—or just to get someone else to want to read it or view it.

But what about how the logline sounds? Let's explore what other elements are involved in a top-notch logline.

Chapter 14

The Voice

I'VE BEEN ASKED ABOUT VOICE BY QUITE A FEW WRITERS over the years. My personal opinion is that if you can give a hint of the voice of your story in the logline, it helps, but it's not a necessity. It's much more important that the three main elements are there and that the length is right, rather than whether or not the sentence adequately reflects the writer's voice. Besides, if the logline has done what it's supposed to do, then your audience will ultimately be reading your full manuscript, which will, of course, give them the absolute best example of your voice.

That said, if your project has a quirky feel or a funny delivery, it's probably a good idea to have that be indicated by your vocabulary choices in your logline. It falls into the category of letting readers know what kind of journey they are in for, one of the main anchors of a good logline. Again, adjusting for voice is not always a necessity, but sometimes it can make enough of a difference that it's worth the effort.

Here's a good example in which I aided a writer in punching up her logline by helping her infuse it with the same humor as her original story:

ORIGINAL

A blonde woman buys and runs a junkyard to earn money to bail her silly brother out of jail.

There's actually nothing specifically wrong with this original logline, and we certainly could have left it as it was, but the original is missing one key thing: It doesn't truly give a feel for how outrageous the writing is. While the logline uses words like "silly" and indicates that there is some comedy involved, I really felt that an overhaul with a bit more of the writer's funny and broad voice could help it out a great deal.

REDO

A big-breasted bombshell bumbles through running a junkyard to earn money to bail her underwear-stealing brother out of jail.

The carefully chosen new vocabulary, along with being much more specific overall, helped give this logline more of the slapstick comedic flair that the original material offers readers. We are now hinting at the voice of the piece because, in this particular case, it's a useful selling tool to let the reader know more about the tone of the material.

Here's another example where I worked with a content creator to focus on the true scariness of his story and emphasize the horror aspect with specific vocabulary choices, in order to make his logline have a much more powerful voice:

ORIGINAL

A college girl is determined to stop the curse in which a spooky house claims the life of a sorority sister every Friday the 13th and turns her into a witch.

This logline is deficient in both the specificity and stakes arenas, but more important, it lacks some carefully chosen horror-based vocabulary, which could give it a stronger selling voice. Here's the rough redone version:

REDO

A college girl must stop undead souls from killing sorority sisters and reincarnating them as cannibalistic witches, or suffer the same fate.

What we essentially did to fix the original sentence was focus the logline's voice on precise elements of the horror genre. I asked the writer to be truly specific about what in the house attacked these girls as well as what happened to them once they were taken. When he revealed that undead souls nabbed the sorority sisters and then reincarnated them as witches who gruesomely ate others, I knew we had to emphasize those creepy elements in order to give the logline a much-needed boost and a stronger voice in its particular genre.

Sometimes, however, honing the voice of the logline isn't about more clearly defining the genre. Many times, the voice of the logline simply comes from concentrating on what makes the project unique. Let's go back to the *Die Hard*-type project at Film Engine:

> *A highly superstitious, world-renowned biological warfare expert must save the president's life armed only with smarts and a four-leaf clover.*

It's the focus on the fact that he's superstitious and therefore carrying around a clover that gives the logline its voice. If I hadn't focused on what made the story different, the voice in the logline wouldn't be clear, because it would sound like just another *Die Hard*-type project.

The voice question is not always only about careful choices or particular vocabulary for flavor, either. It's even more important to make sure that your logline is written with an active voice rather than a passive voice. The difference is this: A passive voice feels like your character is being led through events, while an active voice makes it clear that your protagonist's actions move the plot along. The leads are actually choosing what to do, which in turn pushes the story forward.

Let's explore the difference active rather than passive voice can make to the logline overall. Below is an example of shifting a logline from passive to active voice. The first example, written by a new writer, has much less going for it than the second logline, which we created together:

ORIGINAL

An amnesiac astronaut had vowed to stop an opposing race from annihilating Earth, but he had discovered the aliens had stolen his lost memories and ultimately, he believes he will be forced to choose between completing his quest to recover his memories and working to ensure the survival of the planet.

REDO

An amnesiac astronaut ~~had vowed~~ VOWS to stop an opposing race from annihilating Earth, but ~~he had discovered the aliens had stolen his lost memories and ultimately, he believes he will be forced to~~ MUST choose between ~~completing his quest to~~ recoverING his memories and ~~working to~~ ensureING the PLANET'S survival ~~of the planet~~.

CLEAN

An amnesiac astronaut vows to stop an opposing race from annihilating Earth but must choose between recovering his memories and ensuring the planet's survival.

The redone logline is clearly more powerful, and not just because it's much shorter. The change from passive voice to active voice emphasizes that this is happening right now and is extremely urgent. This is important when marketing your story, as it makes it feel imperative—an essential element when selling a story. The urgency of the action makes what's happening feel significant.

Additionally, it's always of paramount importance to have an active protagonist versus a passive protagonist, since we follow that person throughout the piece. Who wants to invest their time in a character who isn't dynamically leading the process of events along?

Here's another example where we made some shifts from passive voice to active voice:

ORIGINAL

A camera is found by a boy who discovers that deadly images were taken and he wants to figure out why, and wants to try to fix it, before everyone he's taken a snapshot of ends up deceased.

REDO

~~A camera is found by~~ *a boy* FINDS A CAMERA ~~who discovers~~ *that* PRODUCES *deadly images* ~~were taken~~ *and* ~~he wants to~~ MUST *figure out why,* *and* ~~wants to try to~~ *fix it,* *before everyone* ~~he's taken a~~ IN THE *snapshot*S *of ends up* dead.

CLEAN

A boy finds a camera that produces deadly images and must figure out why and fix it before everyone in the snapshots ends up dead.

The redone logline is obviously more powerful, but why? First of all, the camera isn't "found by the boy;" the boy "finds" the camera. (The boy is the protagonist, not the camera.) The active participation involved in finding something rather than simply allowing it to be found is what makes all the difference. Additionally, deadly images weren't "taken"—*past* tense. Instead, the camera "produces"—*present* tense—deadly images. These images are being created right now, not eons ago. Overall, these may seem like subtle changes and shifts, but re-read the two versions of the same logline:

ORIGINAL

A camera is found by a boy who discovers that deadly images were taken and he wants to figure out why, and wants to try to fix it, before everyone he's taken a snapshot of ends up deceased.

REDO

A boy finds a camera that produces deadly images and must figure out why and fix it before everyone in the snapshots ends up deceased.

You can easily see the difference. Better results occur when these changes are made, because they give both the events and the actions immediacy, so the import of what is happening is front and center.

In the end, though, it's most important that you spend your time focusing on ending up with a single tight sentence that highlights what distinguishes your story from others in the same genre, and is as powerful as you can make it. If you do that, then worrying about the voice becomes less of an issue.

To this point, we've gotten through the basic steps for creation of a top-notch, one-sentence selling tool like no other. Now we need to concentrate our efforts on finessing. Attaining a great marketing tool is all about that final important push to make the logline just that much tighter and just that much better.

Chapter 15

Finessing

ONCE YOU GET THE STRUCTURE OF YOUR LOGLINE IN shape, it is important to work on taking it from rough draft to final by further tweaking the vocabulary and picking more dynamic words that add to the overall drama. For example, writing that a character "wants to" do something is okay, but writing that a character is "desperate to" do something adds a sense of urgency that the logline would otherwise lack. Making changes of this nature can help you sell your tale as an exciting journey. Your word choices during the logline creation process, just as when you write your story, can strongly influence the reader, so it's worth the time to carefully finesse and polish until your logline has the most possible impact.

Consider the ways you might describe what's going on in your story. A "poor" man is just someone without funds, but a "destitute" man is someone who is so broke that he is at the end of his rope, which is more dynamic and more powerful. Someone who is "building" a machine is just a person assembling something, but someone who is "creating" a machine is crafting or inventing something, which sounds more unique and makes the character come across as imaginative. If someone "holds on to" an object, they are just keeping it, but if they are "hoarding" that same object, it conveys more worth, because it's something that feels like it's being guarded and valued in some way. I am always surprised by what one deceptively simple word change can do to the perception of certain elements in a story.

I had a project at one time called *The Amazing Days of Abby Hayes*, based on the 22-book series by Anne Mazer. Here's an example of an early draft of the logline I crafted for it, though I knew it still needed some additional finessing:

> *A young girl in a family of geniuses must find the one thing she is good at, or resign herself to a life of ordinariness.*

It was tough to find a way for the journey to sound dynamic, since the stakes are not exactly life and death. But after finessing it for a while, "find" became "uncover," and I added the word "special" to show how difficult the search would be. I also changed "is good at" to "excels at," both because it was shorter (remember, ten dollars per word) and because it raised the stakes. Lastly, I switched "ordinariness" to "insignificance" because it seemed more extreme and therefore more powerful. Compare the two examples, just one draft apart:

ORIGINAL

A young girl in a family of geniuses must find the one thing she is good at, or resign herself to a life of ordinariness.

REDO

A young girl in a family of geniuses must UNCOVER the one SPECIAL thing she EXCELS at, or resign herself to a life of INSIGNIFICANCE.

As you can see here, a little finessing has made a big difference to the overall perception of the protagonist's journey. *Never underestimate the power of changing even one word.*

For those of you paying attention, you might be wondering why I left in the word "young." This story has a strong family dynamic, so it was important for the reader to understand that Abby is the youngest in her family pecking order, because that element soundly affects how she sees herself. Her character's main weakness (and what motivates her journey) is that because she's the youngest she continuously compares her own accomplishments to those of the older members of her family. Thus, in this instance, the adjective was just too important to cut.

Here's another great example of finessing. I had what I thought was my final logline for this family film, but I still felt like there was something missing. It just didn't have the impact I was hoping for. See what happened when I changed only a few words:

ORIGINAL

A baker has dough that comes to life, but once it rises he can't control what he's made, which puts his town at risk.

REDO

A baker CREATES dough that comes to life, but once it rises he can't control THE WILD ANIMALS he's made, which puts his ENTIRE town IN PERIL.

"Creates" is a strong word, because it implies that there was some imagination or invention involved in the process. I chose to be more specific about what the baker made by adding "the wild animals," since I felt that it gave a better picture of the danger to the town. I also used "entire town" for the scope (and therefore impact) it added. Lastly, I switched "at risk" to "in peril" because that made the logline more dramatic.

Here's another example of some necessary tweaking. A content creator brought me a great version of her logline after attending one of my seminars at Grub Street's Muse and the Marketplace. I was impressed with her changes, but I was even more impressed that, as good as it was, she still wanted me to show her how to make it stronger. So we took the time to sit down at lunch and do some little final changes. Below, you can see what a difference that extra half hour of work made to the overall logline.

ORIGINAL

An amputee wants to climb Mount Kilimanjaro, a journey during which every other member of her family has died before.

REDO

A LEG amputee IS DETERMINED to climb Mount Kili-manjaro, a journey THAT ALREADY KILLED BOTH HER PARENTS AND SISTER.

By being specific about the protagonist's injury (*leg* amputee) the revised logline more powerfully underscores the difficulties inherent in climbing that mountain. It's not that the word "amputee" by itself doesn't show that as well, but by adding the leg element it highlights an even greater degree of difficulty. Additionally, explicitly mentioning "her parents and her sister" rather than the amorphous "every other member of her family" gives more emotion and meaning to the journey because now we get a little sense of how close she was to these folks who perished undertaking the same dangerous expedition. Remember, you can never go wrong by being more specific when it comes to your logline.

During the finessing step is also the time to take another look at the length of your sentence and really ask yourself if anything else can be taken out, if there is any way to shorten it, even by a single word. Here's an example from which I took out just a tiny bit of excess text, but it made the logline shorter and tighter, and therefore more impactful:

ORIGINAL

A baby-crazy woman breaks into a local sperm bank and attempts to impregnate herself with the samples before the police can arrest her.

REDO

A baby-crazy woman breaks into a ~~local~~ sperm bank and attempts to impregnate herself ~~with the samples~~ before the police ~~can~~ arrest her.

CLEAN

A baby-crazy woman breaks into a sperm bank and attempts to impregnate herself before police arrest her.

The initial logline was good, but the final is better. And if I had to do a quick pitch of this property to an exec while in a meeting or walking to lunch, I'd much rather pitch the clean redo than my longer original.

Finessing is the final part of the logline creation process, and sometimes the changes are relatively small, but I find that it always makes a very big difference to the overall logline in the end. By taking the time to finesse, you could quite possibly turn a "maybe I'll read it" into a solid "yes."

Chapter 16

Usage

WELL, YOU'VE GONE THROUGH THE PROCESS AND you've finally got a top-notch logline under your belt. So what do you do with it? Most importantly, memorize it. That way, the next time you are at a backyard barbecue with a friend, in an elevator with an executive, or a room at a writers' conference filled with literary agents, when someone asks the standard question, "What is your story about?" you've got the perfect answer ready to go. Trust me, you'll be thanking me when you've managed to pop out a great answer to the most frequently asked, most dreaded question content creators face.

There have been times when I've been out at a business lunch and run into a network executive at the same restaurant. They are with a fellow exec or a show-runner (usually the head writer) or even an actor, and they suddenly say something like, "Hey, what was that cool project you pitched me about the astronaut stuck on that dead planet?" At that moment, I'm eternally grateful to have the logline for the project memorized so I can bring it out to entice them—believe me, they definitely don't want to hear me stumble through a long-winded plot summary during lunch. I think that's one reason I love loglines so much: aside from their marketability they take away the panic that can come when someone puts you on the spot.

Many people are under the impression that a logline is like a pitch, and in a sense it is. But it's much shorter, very dynamic, and more powerful, as it only focuses on what makes the project special. Therefore, this "pitch" can be used in a multitude of places. For example, your new logline now gives you the perfect start to any query letter you may be writing to agents, editors, or publishers in the process of getting your work seen. It tells them what kind of a story they are in for, who the protagonist is, what that person wants, and what is at stake if they do not achieve their goal. Most importantly, it encourages the powers-that-be to keep reading the rest of your query letter, because you've already sold them on the fact that you have a unique and fresh concept to share.

It's becoming increasingly vital to grab an agent's attention fast. Literary agents field hundreds of queries every day, so if you can make yours stand out with the use of a fabulous logline at the top, you're ahead of the game. And you've made their job easier at the same time, letting them know exactly what is exciting and special about what they are going to be reading from you.

A logline can also be used verbally, as I mentioned above, to excite any person who asks that ever-so-daunting question, "What's your story/project about?" I include "project" because, realistically, it doesn't matter whether it's a feature film screenplay, a book, an article, a play, a TV pilot, or just an idea: a logline can be created in exactly the same way and is always your greatest marketing tool.

Recently, agents have been calling me on the phone and reading me loglines from pitch letters they've received. I absolutely love when they do that. First of all, it shows me that loglines work, and it shows respect for my time, because they are not babbling on about the plot. Instead, they are telling me cleanly and concisely what the project is about and why I might be interested. Secondly, their pitch emphasizes how loglines provide them with a terrific tool for selling me on producing their material for adaptation.

Speaking of pitching material, there's a great difference for me now in a room with studio or network executives, as opposed to when I first started. In the beginning, I spent quite a bit of time setting up the underlying material, the character, and the story, trying to get them to see what I could see in it: the potential for a great feature film, television movie, or series. Sometimes I was successful and sometimes I was not. It was frustrating, to say the least, because I put a great deal of time and effort into each and every pitch. Then I remembered a good friend of mine telling me about her first day in a college class, Communication 101. There were two people drawn on the blackboard, one on the left and one on the right. Above each was a speech bubble. In the first, on the left, the bubble included a heart with an arrow through it. The speech bubble for the figure on the right was blank. At its core, communication (as it was explained to her) is trying to get the image in the first bubble to appear in the second bubble. So I knew that if I could somehow successfully get the vision I had for the project across to those in the room—so they had the same vision—I could make the sale. But how to do that? Loglines have become the perfect way to make that happen.

When I begin with a logline as the very start of my pitch, I've already gotten the exec onto my page, seeing my vision in its most unique and sellable form. Who could want for a better marketing tool than that? Today, it's easier for me to approach a pitch, because I know I'm not going to see a bunch of blank faces or—God forbid—confusion in reaction to what I'm saying. Right away, I'm letting everyone know what journey they'll be on, and I've gotten them excited because the tale sounds fresh and new. I can tell you, from when I was on the listening side of that desk, after numerous pitches day in, day out, executives are always excited to hear something new.

Before I ever set up a pitch, I get the logline ready to go, then call the exec and ask if they are searching for projects in the area in which they had expressed interest when we spoke previously. I ask this because mandates—what the studios and networks are looking for—change all the time. The Hollywood joke is that they change minute-by-minute, but in all truth, they do change quite frequently.

One day I was told that the Disney Channel was looking for ghost-based properties, but a week later, they told me that they no longer wanted ghost projects, that they had just had a new creative meeting and wanted witches instead. When the entertainment industry went through a period of consolidation, such as when ABC and Disney merged, it became harder to find places that were all looking for the same material, since the overall number of buyers decreased. The buyers that remained wanted to stand out in the marketplace by making sure their mandates didn't match anyone else's. Suddenly, there was only one place to take a project, instead of three or four. So now I use the logline as a barometer before I ever develop a full pitch (either alone or with a screenwriter). This saves both time and effort. I always try to tell the executive the logline on the phone to make sure that the story still fits their mandate. Otherwise there is no point wasting my time or a screenwriter's time in crafting anything longer. A logline is an easy way to see if someone is interested in your particular story, and is a time-saver to boot. If the logline is received favorably, I work up a pitch, set a date, and it's off to the races. I also start the in-room pitch with the logline. It serves to remind the listeners of my project, which is important because they've probably had a multitude of other properties pitched to them since my initial call, and I can't just assume that they remember mine.

I've also used loglines with many of the agents who pitch me during Book Expo America, which I attend each year in New York. Upstairs, away from the crowded, Costco-sized booksellers' space on the first floor of the Javits Convention Center, is the rights area, filled with tables helmed by most of the literary agencies on the East Coast. I usually spend at least a day or two table-hopping through appointments to find out about new books or proposals coming down the pike. Much of that time is taken up by listening to pitches from the agents about their content. I then get to ask for some clarification. Little do they know that the questions I pose are leading them toward a more concise pitch, because they are the exact ones I use to create a logline. I'll ask the agents, for example, "Who is driving the story forward?" "What is the lead character trying to achieve?" "What are they worried about happening if they don't get it?" "Would the story work just as well with an adult lead instead of a teen lead?" Answering these types of queries will help them for their next pitch with whoever has the appointment after mine. The questions are also incredibly beneficial to me, because they help me better understand the story and determine if I think it has the hook needed to set it up as an adaptation project. And if so, I now also have much of the information I need to create a nice logline for the work.

I've also used loglines with screenwriters I'm working with to help them more fully focus their pitches for the studios or networks. Occasionally, when they pitch me what they'll be saying in the room, there may be some great elements, but much of the content seems to be either unclear or missing something. The only way to fix it, as far as I'm concerned, is to talk about the logline with them. For many screenwriters, learning how to generate a logline as a way to focus their pitch is something new, but usually they end up adopting it for their other projects as well.

I have a children's project with a talented screenwriter who has only done television projects to date, but our upcoming pitch is for a big theatrical feature film with an animation component. We'll be pitching it to Sony Pictures Animation, among others. When I asked the writer what the logline would be, she gave me this:

Two orphan sisters discover that fairy tales are real when they have to rescue their long-lost aunt from a giant and save a town their family is sworn to protect.

While that's not a bad first logline, it was clear to me that the world of the story is just too small; it feels very TV. If this story is going to end up on the big screen, the stakes have to be raised, big-time. It could no longer be a story about two little girls and their aunt in a fairy-tale town. The whole world needed to be at risk, because feature films are usually looked at in terms of big screen equals big world creation and big stakes. After the screenwriter and I discussed the story at length and tossed around some ideas about what elements could be changed, here's the rough draft we created as a jumping-off point:

Two orphan sisters have to stop giants determined to escape the confines of their fairy-tale land and unleash destruction on the world.

There's a pretty big difference from the original, and the screenwriter was able to go back and apply these new, higher stakes to her pitch. Suddenly, everything mattered more, and the story she told was more focused because she knew what the ultimate goal was: stop the giants from destroying the world. That's a big idea and therefore definitely feels right for a feature film rather than television. What I love about this logline-based approach is that it's quite possible the exec in the room would have said something vague like "I liked the pitch but I think the story needs to feel bigger," and we would have left without a sale, wondering what exactly he meant. Instead, we've gotten right to the heart of it by employing logline creation techniques, and can now go into the pitch knowing we've already taken care of the "up the stakes" issue ahead of time. Hopefully, it will result in setting up the property at the studio.

If you think about it, in much of life, loglines are already in use. The television series *Shark Tank* has up-and-coming inventors start their product pitches to the sharks with a solid logline. Most news anchors preview their coming stories with a logline before the commercial break so that the viewer will be intrigued and want to tune back in afterward. Even successful Twitter campaigns, at only 140 characters, are essentially great examples of top-notch loglines. At home, a good bedtime story starts with what is essentially a logline, as does any terrific story told at a dinner party. At work, a pitch to your boss usually starts with a good logline, as does a salacious recap of a favorite show around the water cooler in the break room. If you look around, you'll find that loglines are used absolutely everywhere, so the value of gaining the skill set to create a perfect logline is truly ineffable.

Recently, in an online article for CNN, I was touted as "the Book Whisperer" of Hollywood. I think a more accurate assessment would have been if they had described me as "the Logline Whisperer," because none of the multitudes of book projects I've been lucky enough to set up would have happened without the first step being the creation of a tight and powerful logline.

Chapter 17

Fiction vs. Nonfiction/Memoir

NOW THAT WE'VE BROKEN DOWN THE LOGLINE INTO ITS most basic elements, I think it's important to discuss fiction versus nonfiction, since it's something I get asked about quite a bit by writers when they approach me after one of my seminars. They want to know if these principles can be applied only to imaginary material or if they work just as well with true stories. To date I've set up five memoir projects and have three more currently out in the marketplace, so the answer is that loglines absolutely work just as well in the nonfiction arena.

I think that the toughest thing about nonfiction is that true story and memoir writers are too close to their material. Many times, this results in a "can't see the forest for the trees" scenario. It's the same thing that happens when a film is written and directed by the same person. Rarely does this result in a great feature film. Don't get me wrong, there are a handful of folks (like Kenneth Branagh, for example) who do this quite well, but for the most part, this lack of perspective ends up being a disaster. The tough part is that when you are that close to your material, it's hard to see what's needed in order to sell it. I try to always have the writer look at the work dispassionately, as if someone else wrote it, as if they are telling someone else's story, to sort of give them "new eyes" that aren't clouded by their own experiences. If they can do that, then they can focus on the anchors of the logline in a way that will garner them the results they desire.

At one of my many speaking engagements, a gentleman asked me about a logline for his fitness work. I asked him what made his work different from the thousands of other fitness books out there, and he told me that he was revolutionizing fitness training for senior citizens. I asked him specifically how he was accomplishing that and he talked about the idea of not treating them as "breakables" but as older humans who therefore had had a lifetime of fitness experience under their belts already. I loved how unique that sounded, and after playing around with those elements for a while, I told him that his logline should be something like this:

> From the creator of the new "Unbreakable" training method, a revolutionary guide to senior fitness.

See how cool that sounds? As you can see, for a nonfiction work, the same principles apply with regard to highlighting what makes it most unique. Even someone with 50 fitness books on their shelf may now pick this one up for themselves or for a beloved grandparent.

Memoirs can present a particular challenge, since they sometimes lack the inherent drama found in most fictional works, and yet the fact that they are true stories is exactly what makes them highly sellable. The ability to promote a project based on the idea that this event or that person is real is honestly invaluable. So how do you tackle this issue, when you have true personal stories but without the "umph" found in most fictional dramatic material? Following are some examples of projects I've developed based on actual people and events. I've highlighted my different approaches to generating loglines for each of them.

The first property tells the true story of an American contractor who, through a series of circumstances, spent almost a year as a prisoner in Iraq. It's the story of his kidnapping, captivity, and rescue, and is a powerful tale, to be sure, but what makes it different from any other POW story in the marketplace already? How could I make it sound like a standout? There are literally thousands of POW tales. So, as I would with any fiction-based material, I ultimately had to focus on the specifics of what made it unique. I determined that it was the perspective-changing scope of the circumstances that made this a standout property. Here's the rough logline:

> In this true story, a contractor spends 311 days imprisoned in a four-foot high concrete cell underground before becoming one of the only US hostages ever rescued from Iraq.

It's the new and different information given, that the contractor was in a tiny box underground for 311 days and is one of the only people who ever survived such incarceration, which makes this story truly exceptional and therefore highly marketable. The fact that it's a true story is definitely a selling tool, but by emphasizing these dramatic circumstances I pushed the elements that make the story unique. There may be many other stories about POWs in Iraq, but none of them will have the exact same circumstances as this gentleman. That is why I keep pushing the idea of being specific when you write a logline, because it is those very details that make the story different and special.

The second property, which I initially set up with Scott Stuber at NBC and is now with Mike Medavoy, tells of a lawyer/law professor with a sociopathic mind and the ability to mimic those around her in order to put on a façade of emotions she never actually feels. (I mentioned this project earlier.) As groundbreaking as this work is, and despite the fact that the woman herself is an unbelievably charismatic and dynamic person, the toughest thing about this piece was figuring out a way to overcome the fact that most folks who hear "sociopath" think of crazed killers. So the focus became not so much on the fact that she was a lawyer/law professor/sociopath, but how to tap into the black humor of the piece so that she could be a *likable* lawyer sociopath. After all, if you can't root for the protagonist, you don't have a show, and you certainly can't make a sale. Here's the rough logline:

> *A sociopath attorney's success is due to her emotionless approach to life, but when it kills her promotion, she has to do the unthinkable—learn how to be a nice person.*

Likability is one of the most important elements for a property to sell, and the word "sociopath"—its best selling tool—also became this story's biggest liability. So it was important to focus the logline on the dark comedy inherent in the text so that particular marketing hurdle could be quickly and easily overcome. Ironically, the purpose of the book was to redefine the idea of what a sociopath is, and yet it was that exact misconception which initially made it so hard to sell for adaptation.

Another property I really struggled with was the life story of a woman who ran three strip clubs in New York City. While it is unusual for a female to be in the successful position of general manager in that highly male-dominated industry (and Bishop-Lyons Entertainment was simultaneously working on a reality show to prove it), I just didn't feel that was enough to sell the property. But I was stumped. It seemed like that element was truly all there was to the story. So what was missing?

As a result, I decided to revamp my thinking on the project. I tried to think of this memoir as an imaginary story, no longer bogged down by the realities of true life. If that were what I had to work with, and she were the protagonist in a fictional piece, what would she want? What was propelling this journey? What came to mind was incredibly helpful in crafting the logline, as it helped me determine what was needed. Here's the rough draft logline I created:

> *The true story of the only female GM of the highest-echelon strip club in NY, and her desperate search for a man to love her unconditionally.*

Her journey is an incredible one, but her goal in life wasn't to become the general manager of a strip club. What she truly wanted was to find the perfect guy, which as you can imagine is difficult in that dark world (as those are not the kind of men who frequent stripper establishments). She's pursuing the improbable and possibly the impossible; that's why we will care about her and root for her, just as if she were a fictional character.

As mentioned earlier, the most difficult part of true stories is that their writers know the facts. They become so tied to each and every part of the actual people, places, and events in their content that they can't separate themselves enough to realize that all stories require some bit of embellishment or creative license. As a result, they are often (and naturally) upset by the adaptation process, because it *always* involves making adjustments to their original story. Sometimes, it involves so many changes that the literary credit changes from "based on" to "inspired by." It's one of the reasons why I can sell projects only with partials or proposals rather than full manuscripts. So much is going to change from book to screen that it becomes unimportant how much of the manuscript you have available as long as what you do have introduces the characters and the writing, and of course shows where the story is going.

Film, as a visual medium, will always call for necessary adjustments to the underlying written material to accommodate the difference between word and screen. I remember how much I enjoyed working with Sandra Brown on the adaptation of *The Witness*, because she really understood what was needed for reworking what was in her original novel. Anytime we were on a call and would discuss a situation where something worked in her story but was essentially in the character's head, Sandra would say something like, "I realize that that works in the book but probably won't work for film—let me see if I can come up with something more visual for the movie adaptation." It was an absolute pleasure to have an author who was so attuned to the differences from page to screen. That's rarely the case, however, so it's incredibly important to have a producer (like myself) or an agent who understands how difficult adaptations can be, who can guide a writer through the changes step-by-step.

The fact that material is a true story or a memoir isn't enough to market it to the entertainment industry, because with that classification as its sole selling tool, it sounds like many other stories in the same arena. You also come up against the erroneous assumption that these types of properties innately lack drama because they are not fictional stories from a writer's creative mind. What's amazing about a logline is that with all of these caveats working against the material, a perfectly crafted sentence is able to give nonfiction and memoir material the extra boost it badly needs to make it unbelievably sellable. And while loglines are always used for fiction material, sometimes seeing nonfiction and memoir work in that same light and gaining the perspective of forgetting "it's all true" can help you craft your perfect sentence.

Many nonfiction authors tell me that they are just writing their stories down to get them on paper and share their experiences with others. They don't really know what in particular makes it different than other content in the same arena, except that it's their personal story. My answer is always the same. That's not enough to sell it—and if you do not know what makes your story unique, you shouldn't be writing it.

Chapter 18

It's All About the Drama

GEORGES POLTI, A FRENCH WRITER OF THE LATE 1800s and early 1900s, famously created a list of 36 dramatic situations, designed to categorize every situation that might happen in a story. While I'm not sure I completely agree with all of Polti's ideas, his basic suggestion is that every circumstance is an offshoot of one of these 36 scenarios. If so, then the challenge becomes making anything at all sound unique with only 36 basic choices, especially those stories that feel like something we've heard before.

Currently, I have quite a few projects in the pipeline that some might consider less-sensational fare. These are projects that fall smack-dab into one of those 36 situations. I want to take a moment to talk about them, because sometimes there's a sense that properties which seem to inherently lack dynamic drama can't be given a hook with which to sell them. As discussed regarding memoir and nonfiction works, however, that is simply not the case. With some work and creativity, any property can be given a strong marketing hook.

My first example is a property about a woman who, after a 23-year marriage, was left by her husband not because of another woman (the typical scenario) but because he found out that he had inoperable cancer. Suddenly, the man had a need to squeeze every ounce of life out of every minute of each remaining day that he had left, and she just didn't fit into that plan. Sadly, cancer is not a new topic, nor is separation or divorce after many years of marriage. Additionally, the death of their marriage was accomplished with a minimum of fuss and a complete lack of fireworks or theatrics. So how can a creative and powerful logline be achieved from such lackluster beginnings?

The answer lies in focusing on the twist, or unexpected element, because that is the only drama available. Typically, in a situation where a man is leaving a woman after years of marriage, the first thought is always that there is another woman involved—a mistress. That's what's expected. However, in this case, the other woman is actually cancer. So that became the meat of the new logline. Here's the rough draft:

A woman struggles to fight against the pull of her husband's new mistress—cancer.

Now the story sounds intriguing, right? I took something that made this story seem like one of a million others and turned it on its ear. This is a perfect logline at work: it takes a story that is deficient in some essential drama (because it lacks uniqueness) and twists it to seem somehow new again.

I always tell writers to focus on what is unique about their stories. (In fact, I've probably used the word unique overmuch in this book!) The pervading thought is that if you can't find that element, you don't have a marketing tool, and a majority of the time that's true. However, as you can see from my previous example, occasionally doing the complete opposite—thinking about what makes it expected—can help you come up with a way to actually make it unique. Cool, huh?

Another example is the story of a successful career woman, with a childhood trauma, who made the slow spiral into drugs and alcohol due to intense stress. If it sounds like you've heard this story before, you probably have. It's not a new tale, nor is there much to make it shine amongst the multitude of other stories in this same arena. That said, a strong logline can still help this piece stand out from the pack and make an impact in the marketplace. But where to start?

To me, the uniqueness of this story comes out only when focusing on the drama inherent in extreme perspective. It's a technique I fall back on a lot; it works very much in the vein of the "one grain of rice can tip the scale" idea. This woman was very high up: a powerful, achieving moneymaker who had it all together, until a seemingly insignificant and suppressed memory changed everything. From having the world to having nothing at all because of only one small thing—now *that* is the basis of a good, strong logline. Here's the rough draft:

> A powerful executive plummets into a drugged-out, near-death state because of a long-forgotten trauma: the murder of her newborn sister.

By centering the logline on the extremes of changing from a very successful executive to a bottom-of-the-barrel druggie due to one simple memory, I've given it the pressure-cooker feel that it needs. I've provided an emotional hook where there really was none, because the story is one we've heard before. By concentrating my logline only on the far ends of the spectrum, I was able to create a strong perspective and give the story resonance.

In both of the previous illustrations, the path to the logline stemmed from finding the tiniest grain of drama, whether by twisting an expected element into something unexpected, or by steering the story toward an extreme perspective and exploiting it to the fullest. It's the drama that sells the story's excitement, so you have to mine for it wherever you can. But what do you do if neither of these approaches works for your particular tale?

There's a final tool that I sometimes resort to using to create some punch when there are no other options open to me. This usually occurs either due to the lack of specificity (because of the type of story it is) or the fact that it's a familiar tale that doesn't lend itself to the creative logline generation options I've mentioned previously. It is a process I like to call word-flipping, and it involves changing the order of things (and a bit of vocabulary) to dramatic effect. Here's a rough example:

ORIGINAL

A bum spends his life on the street trying unsuccessfully to regain the job that he had before the booze took it away.

This logline is okay, but it's all about what the man has lost, so it sounds like a depressingly familiar story. It lacks a hook.

There's no twist to be mined in this situation, nor is there any extreme perspective to a homeless man looking for a job. In this particular instance, then, a bit of word-flipping (along with some choice vocabulary changes) can help make this logline much more vibrant.

REDO

The booze ruined him, so a street bum fights to regain the job that can provide a new life.

As you can see, the word order has been shifted a bit. It's not a huge adjustment overall, and more work is needed, but it's enough of a change that there are suddenly dynamics which weren't there in the first iteration, and which thankfully make it infinitely more sellable.

Although it does work, word-flipping should always be a last resort, because it puts the protagonist in a subordinate position rather than in the powerful position at the front of the logline, and that is not typically a helpful shift. However, when there is no other drama to be had, this little trick can provide a much-needed tool to give your sentence some power.

As we now know, the whole point of a great logline is to be able to market your story quickly and effectively, and the main ingredient in being able to do that is drama. So, realistically, however you can unearth that valuable commodity, it's worth the time and effort to do so.

Chapter 19

The Logline Process

ALTHOUGH THIS ALL STARTS TO SEEM FAIRLY EASY AS I break it down for you into its core elements, it took me years to acquire the skills needed to create a great logline. Even now, with the thousands of examples I've produced over time, it's all about revising and rewriting. Honestly, sometimes it takes me a few days and fifteen to twenty fairly bad versions before I finally end up with something workable.

Sometimes walking away, going to work on something else, and then coming back to the logline fresh and with a new perspective changes everything for the better. I do this frequently when I get frustrated at not being able to whip the logline into the shape I think it should be in. I take a walk, go get a coffee, or even ignore the logline for a few days by working on something else entirely. So go ahead, start with ten sentences or even a crazy-long run-on sentence. Approach, walk away, and then re-approach your logline days or even weeks later. As long as it ultimately ends up as a concise one-liner that you are happy with after all of your drafts, you've done a terrific job!

At this time, I think it would be helpful to go through a step-by-step example of the creative process I go through in crafting one of my loglines. Let's start with a fiction example.

VERSION 1

A man with a background in the military travels all over the world, where he ends up saving others in order to save himself.

So, as usual, the first version isn't very good—in fact it's pretty terrible. However, a good friend cautioned me when I was looking for my first home not to wait for the perfect house but to "just jump in" to the real estate market. It was good advice, because in reality you are never going to find the perfect house, only homes you want to fix up and make the way you want them to be. In the same fashion, if I waited for my logline to be perfect, I'd still be sitting with my hand silently hovering over the keyboard, staring at an empty page. So instead, I write down whatever I can think of about the story that's in my brain. I know it will need tons of work but it gets me started and that's the goal. Here's the next iteration:

VERSION 2

An international man of mystery with a military back-ground travels the world saving others in order to save himself.

Adding a silly phrase like "an international man of mystery" makes it clear that I was feeling like the logline needed some punch, a little more interest, but I went too far. This feels almost soap opera-esque—so it's back to the drawing board. Here's the next version:

VERSION 3

A troubled ex-military man travels the world to avoid his own personal demons, but in the process saves others, which helps him save himself.

As you can see, I was trying to give more of a feel for the protagonist by writing that he was "troubled," which isn't great, but makes the sentence better than it was. Also, I added "ex-military" because it helped convey that the character is a bit rogue but has skills. Lastly, I was trying to bring in information about what was driving him on this journey, but "personal demons" is just too general a concept. Here's my next attempt:

VERSION 4

A troubled ex-Navy Seal exorcises his own personal demons by spending his life traveling the world to save others.

Here, I tried to make the demons more personal and get even more specific about the man by stating that he was a Navy Seal. But I wasn't sure how much this really helped me, as it's still at the same level of drama. I also expanded upon his journey by mentioning how much of his time is taken up by the pursuit for salvation, which improves upon the previous version slightly. Here's the next version:

VERSION 5

A troubled ex-Navy Seal fights his own personal demons by forcing himself to travel the world saving the lives of strangers.

I thought that switching to more powerful vocabulary like "fights" and "forcing" would help give the sentence some much-needed drama. I also wanted the generic "others" to become the more defined "strangers." At this point, it's creeping closer to a decent logline. Here's the next try:

VERSION 6

An emotionally damaged ex-Navy Seal fights his inner demons, in penance by traveling the world saving the lives of strangers.

I wasn't really happy with "troubled," because it's too vague, so I switched it in this version to "emotionally damaged." I'm trying to get a description of the man that more fully expresses his state of mind, while also trying to hint at what is motivating him. I also added the "penance," thinking that might help with motivation, but ended up taking it right back out in the next draft because it's too vague a concept—and as we know, loglines are all about specifics. Here's my next iteration:

VERSION 7

An emotionally damaged ex-Navy Seal fights inner demons by traveling the world in pursuit of saving the lives of strangers.

Well, I cut some words (including "penance") simply because, at ten dollars per word, they weren't helping me. This version is tighter but overall not that much better, though it does have the protagonist actively pursuing ("in pursuit of") something, and active voice is always helpful. That said, I knew I needed to make some much more drastic changes, as I was seven versions in and still far from my goal of a good logline. So, after taking some time away from working on this sentence to get some perspective, here's the next version I came up with:

VERSION 8

A degenerate ex-Seal fights inner demons by forcing himself to continuously save the lives of complete strangers.

"Degenerate" was probably a poor choice, as it gives him a sinister edge that I didn't want, but I was still toying with vocabulary that would allow the reader to understand the character's heart and motivations. I also cut out "Navy" because it didn't add anything, and most people will get that from the word "Seal." He's "forcing himself" here, which was my attempt to infuse some of the drama I felt was still missing. He's also saving other people's lives "continuously," as I wanted it to feel like he was driven . . . but I was still unhappy with the logline overall. Here's the next version, after I took yet another short break from it:

VERSION 9

A bottomed-out ex-Seal fights inner demons by forcing himself to continuously save the lives of complete strangers.

With the phrase "bottomed-out," I finally have a description of the protagonist that I like. It shows that he is on the bottom rung emotionally, so (1) you can see where he is starting from at the beginning of his journey and (2) you can understand why he is doing what he is doing for these people. But I still felt that there was something missing. I thought about this for quite a while and then realized the thing that was missing: the stakes. What does he have to lose if he does not remain along this path? So I added in some information, without adding a ton of word count, to tell the reader what would happen if he did not continue pursuing his journey:

VERSION 10

A bottomed-out ex-Seal fights to overcome his suicidal tendencies by continuously saving the lives of complete strangers.

By including "suicidal tendencies," I was able to show that if the protagonist did not continue to save others he would end up emotionally bankrupt and take his own life. This was the vital ingredient that had been missing throughout the generation process. While my other adjustments were necessary along the way, this change is the one that finally brought the logline to life. Once I'd included what was at stake, my logline was complete.

Here are all of the versions again, without my commentary, so you can follow the step-by-step progression:

VERSION 1

A man with a background in the military travels all over the world, where he ends up saving others in order to save himself.

VERSION 2

An international man of mystery with a military background travels the world saving others in order to save himself.

VERSION 3

A troubled ex-military man travels the world to avoid his own personal demons, but in the process saves others, which helps him save himself.

VERSION 4

A troubled ex-Navy Seal exorcises his own personal demons by spending his life traveling the world to save others.

VERSION 5

A troubled ex-Navy Seal fights his own personal demons by forcing himself to travel the world saving the lives of strangers.

VERSION 6

An emotionally damaged ex-Navy Seal fights his inner demons, in penance by traveling the world saving the lives of strangers.

VERSION 7

An emotionally damaged ex-Navy Seal fights inner demons by traveling the world in pursuit of saving the lives of strangers.

VERSION 8

A degenerate ex-Seal fights inner demons by forcing himself to continuously save the lives of complete strangers.

VERSION 9

A bottomed-out ex-Seal fights inner demons by forcing himself to continuously save the lives of complete strangers.

VERSION 10

A bottomed-out ex-Seal fights to overcome his suicidal tendencies by continuously saving the lives of complete strangers.

That's a long process, right? And honestly, that's nothing. I've had projects that went through twenty or thirty revisions (or more). But if you take a moment to reread the first logline and then the last one, skipping the ones in between, you'll see why it's all worth it:

VERSION 1

A man with a background in the military travels all over the world, where he ends up saving others in order to save himself.

VERSION 10

A bottomed-out ex-Seal fights to overcome his suicidal tendencies by continuously saving the lives of complete strangers.

See what a difference a few hours over a few different days makes? This worked and reworked logline will sell the content to a buyer in a way that the first version never could have done. Now let's explore the process using a nonfiction example.

VERSION 1

An egotistical lifetime beauty pageant winner suddenly learns the realities of life when a tragedy forces her to shift careers into law enforcement.

This isn't the best starting logline I've ever created but, as I mentioned earlier, it's really important just to get something down on paper, to get going on the process. I know I need to cross out "egotistical" because, at ten dollars per word, it doesn't help me sell. Additionally, this woman's story is true and rather unique—going from winning pageant crowns to fighting the good fight on the mean streets—so it's clear to me that a lot is missing right now, because this logline makes her journey sound a bit ho-hum. Usually that comes from being too general, so that's what I focused on for my first revision.

VERSION 2

A lifetime beauty pageant winner suddenly learns a life lesson when her son's death forces her to shift careers into law enforcement.

I'm not sure why I thought "life lesson" was better than "realities of life," because it's just as general, but this was only my second pass at the logline, so I'll try not to be too hard on myself. Changing the "tragedy" to "her son's death" has helped quite a bit, however, because it's infinitely more specific. Let's look at the next iteration.

VERSION 3

A beauty pageant winner suddenly destroyed by her son's death forces her to shift careers into law enforcement.

Notice I removed "lifetime," because I didn't think it was helping me sell the story: It made the character sound old. If you've spent a lifetime at something, you are probably getting up there in age. Additionally, that word made it seem like she's only making the change into law at the end of her life, which wasn't true. So "lifetime" definitely had to be cut. I also removed "learns a life lesson" because it was much too general, and I felt that the emphasis needed to be put on what caused her to make the big occupation change—her son's death—hence the addition of "destroyed by." Here's the next one:

VERSION 4

A beauty pageant winner is destroyed by her son's death, which forces her to pursue joining the SWAT team.

I changed "suddenly destroyed" to "is destroyed" in order to bring the sentence into present tense and make it sound more immediate. "Suddenly" works as well, but I try different things when crafting successive drafts, to see what feels right. I knew that I had to change "shift careers into law enforcement," because it made it sound like she simply veered into another line of work. That's truly what was making it sound boring. It also lacked specificity, which I finally acquired by introducing the SWAT team.

VERSION 5

A beauty queen is destroyed by her son's death, which forces her to pursue joining the SWAT team.

"Beauty pageant winner" was too many words for a logline at ten dollars per word, so I switched it to "beauty queen." But I knew I could make it even tighter before looking for what else could be amped up.

VERSION 6

A beauty queen, destroyed by her son's death, instead pursues joining the SWAT team.

By tightening everything, I can really see what I have and what I don't. It's getting there, but I need to ratchet up the drama somehow. I first tried to give it some power by adding back in some of the motivation I'd taken out.

VERSION 7

In this true story . . . after her son is killed, a beauty queen joins the SWAT team to fight her own depression by making a difference.

I wanted to add that this is a nonfiction story because, as I discussed earlier in this book, it's a good additional selling tool. Also, because it is such a big jump from beauty queen to SWAT team member, I wanted to make sure that the audience understood that the journey was absolutely true. I made "pursues joining" into "joins" instead, in order to make the sentence more active. But adding the motivation in hasn't helped me much, and has made it too long again. So it's back to cutting . . .

VERSION 8

In this true story . . . after her son is killed, a beauty queen joins the SWAT team to fight her own depression.

"Making a difference" is one of those dreadful generalities that just had to go, and I figured the idea of making a difference is already built into the idea of joining a SWAT team anyway. But still, the logline wasn't giving me what I wanted. So I took a couple days' break from revising before looking at it once again. Here's my revision with some new perspective, provided by my time away:

VERSION 9

Destroyed by her son's sudden death, this is the unvarnished true story of one woman's passage from beauty queen to SWAT team.

Oh, what a difference a little bit of a break can make! I used some extreme perspective to emphasize the two far ends of the career scale, which gave it a strong impact. I also went back to my earlier bit about her son and did a little word-flipping as well. I pulled out all of my tricks on this one. I also liked the rhyme of "queen" and "team" when spoken out loud, because it helped accentuate this hook. But now, in revamping, I'd added in some unneeded vocabulary, and I wanted to see if changing any words would help with impact, so it was time to finesse.

VERSION 10

Destroyed by her son's death, this is the true story of one woman's journey from beauty queen to SWAT team.

This feels pretty good to me now, with those final few tweaks. And just to clarify: The stakes are built in by the fact that she is trying to get over her son's death and that joining the SWAT team is obviously her way of doing so. Of course, there are not always ten versions for fiction and nonfiction loglines, and in fact there were quite a few more steps in both of these examples, but I wanted to simplify everything so you could easily follow along. Here are the versions for you without my commentary so you can see the process:

VERSION 1

An egotistical lifetime beauty pageant winner suddenly learns the realities of life when a tragedy forces her to shift careers into law enforcement.

VERSION 2

A lifetime beauty pageant winner suddenly learns a life lesson when her son's death forces her to shift careers into law enforcement.

VERSION 3

A beauty pageant winner suddenly destroyed by her son's death forces her to shift careers into law enforcement.

VERSION 4

A beauty pageant winner is destroyed by her son's death, which forces her to pursue joining the SWAT team.

VERSION 5

A beauty queen is destroyed by her son's death, which forces her to pursue joining the SWAT team.

VERSION 6

A beauty queen, destroyed by her son's death, instead pursues joining the SWAT team.

VERSION 7

In this true story . . . after her son is killed, a beauty queen joins the SWAT team to fight her own depression by making a difference.

VERSION 8

In this true story . . . after her son is killed, a beauty queen joins the SWAT team to fight her own depression.

VERSION 9

Destroyed by her son's sudden death, this is the unvarnished true story of one woman's passage from beauty queen to SWAT team.

VERSION 10

Destroyed by her son's death, this is the true story of one woman's journey from beauty queen to SWAT team.

That's quite a process, but absolutely worth it. Take a look again at the immense difference between the first version and the final version:

VERSION 1

An egotistical lifetime beauty pageant winner suddenly learns the realities of life when a tragedy forces her to shift careers into law enforcement.

VERSION 10

Destroyed by her son's death, this is the true story of one woman's journey from beauty queen to SWAT team.

The most amazing thing about all of this work on both the fiction and nonfiction loglines is that now that I have these two great sentences as selling tools, it will be much easier for me to market these two stories to the industry. These loglines came to life through the process of continuously asking myself the questions we've explored in this book: "What does the protagonist want?" "What makes this journey unique?" "What is at stake?" Only through this diligent course of ongoing thoughtful development will a top-notch logline eventually reveal itself.

Chapter 20

Expanding the Logline

AFTER YOU'VE DEVELOPED A WINNING LOGLINE, YOU'LL need to develop your writing further, extend your piece from that single sentence to a longer version. As awesome as a logline is, you will ultimately, of course, have to expand to a slightly lengthier format. No one is green-lighting anything on only a sentence. But true expansion should occur *after* you create your logline, because this one-sentence wonder can help you determine what's missing from your labors *before* you take the time to write and write and write. And in addition, you now have the perfect guideline to help steer the process as you get down to brass tacks.

When I sell, I always start with a logline—that's a given—but if the logline has done its job and managed to catch the executive's attention, I immediately send over a longer document (one to five pages) to keep the interest flowing. So the initial grab is all about the logline, but then it's about expanding that logline into a longer format to hopefully make the final sale. As an aside, one neat trick I like to employ when writing longer form material is to always end the write-ups at the end of the second act (in filmic three-act structure). That's the moment when the character is at their lowest, when all seems lost and you have no idea how the person will get out of the mess they are in. I like to stop there because it's a terrific cliff-hanger; it leaves the reader wanting more, which is always the reaction you are looking for. Think about it: If you tell the whole story to the very end, then the suspense you've built throughout the tale is now dissipated. Additionally, you've given away the reason for the reader to ask to read the entire work.

Knowing that you ultimately need a longer bit of writing, how can you accomplish that? Where do you start? Well, the good news is that you already have the most important elements in place. You know who your protagonist is, what that person wants, and what is at stake. You've also already focused on what's most unique about your project. How great is it that the main anchors of a successful piece of content are already in place for you? Give a gold star to the logline. Now you need to know how to grow it into slightly longer-form material. To do so, think of your logline like a simple instruction manual, providing you with a step-by-step way to increase the length of your content. With that logline in place, you literally have all of the information you need to run with your idea yet stay on track.

The first piece of the puzzle is defining your protagonist. Well, you've already identified the main character for the logline, so now you need only to put together your list of adjectives that more fully describe him or her. Again, as you've learned from your logline creation, be specific. Don't just write down that they are "funny." Instead decide if they have a dry wit or black humor or a slapstick mentality. Alternatively, are they old school, where they think they're humorous but actually aren't? The more detailed you can be, the better defined your character will be, and the more your reader will be interested in that person's journey.

Additionally, you'll need to examine what main flaw the character has—something we call the lead's Achilles' heel. Is he or she too focused on work and not enough on family? Does he or she have a major gambling problem which affects his or her ability to create a stable marriage? What is the element that is that person's greatest weakness? If you are defining your protagonist, this must be part of that process. Once you've made a long list of adjectives and figured out the Achilles' heel, you've made a good start on sketching out a write-up on your main character.

Now let's discuss how to further develop what that lead character wants. Let's use an example from above. If his or her greatest weakness is being a workaholic, then what that person wants is to spend more meaningful time with their spouse and kids. Additionally, how they might achieve that goal becomes the journey the character is on throughout your work. See how easy it is to formulate your story once the logline is firmly in place?

Now you know how to expand your character description as well as further explore what the lead person is fighting against as well as what they want. All of these elements combined will help lengthen your final write-up, but let's take it one step further. Let's discuss how to further develop part three: what is at stake.

Using the previous example, what is at stake? Well, if the character doesn't manage to find balance and spend more time with family, and less with his or her coworkers, it's a pretty sure bet that that person will lose their family—so the stakes are easily defined and clear. What is at stake if they do not achieve their goal? They will be utterly alone. That's a great basis for a more emotional, lengthier piece to turn on to an interested reader.

Let's take the next example I gave, exploring a character with a gambling problem. The lead is a gambler but not just a simple once-in-a-while gambler. He or she is someone who can't stop, who has a *major* gambling problem—that's your protagonist. What the character wants is to find a way to stop gambling because it's affecting his or her marriage. And what is at stake is if they don't stop gambling? The character will lose his or her spouse to divorce. Thanks to your logline, here's the roadmap for this character's journey throughout the story. Now, as you can see, writing an outline or treatment for this material becomes much, much simpler.

It's also key to note that, as with the logline, every experience this character endures along the way to his or her goal should be active and build with urgency to the end. Don't let him or her be buffeted along from event to event; make sure that everything that happens is a result of that character actively pursuing their goal. With all of these elements in place, you can create a longer form of the material that practically writes itself, because it now has both focus and direction.

Let's take a new logline example and expand it accordingly.

A fat girl invents a weight-loss pill, but when its side effect is stupidity, she must determine what's most important before the pill's changes become permanent.

Based on that logline and what we've discussed in this chapter, here's how to expand. First, what are the built-in descriptive items? Well, the lead character is a rather overweight young woman, and she's obviously very smart, because she's invented a pill to help her drop those nasty pounds. These are two good places to start from when creating your much-lengthier adjective list. Other possibilities can then be added: Maybe she's got a round, apple-cheeked face. You can also expand upon her education, and perhaps whether it kept her from having friends. Maybe she's shy because of it. Whatever you choose, just keep building. And what is her Achilles' heel? That she admits to an insatiable hunger and can't stop eating. There's a good jumping off point for her psychological state, because there must be a reason for why she's like that, and hopefully one that's good for another page or two of diligent writing.

Next, remember what you've learned from the logline generation: What she wants isn't to lose weight. Losing weight is too general. Many characters have pursued that goal, so it feels rather tired. What she really wants is to find a way to choose between being fat and being stupid (a side effect of the pill she's invented). That is much more interesting and unique, and a tough decision to boot. It's certainly something that will keep a reader engaged. This is the defined quest your character is on throughout the creative content you are writing. Added to that, if she doesn't choose properly, she'll be either hugely chubby or a complete idiot forever, which adds the urgency—something a piece of writing always needs.

Notice that every part of this story is expanded from our first simple sentence to a longer form of material; it all comes from the logline itself. Think about what a great base you have to work from! When the characters are well-defined, when what they want is clear and what is at stake is understood, then it's an easy process to build on those elements to create a fully fleshed-out write-up, which people are going to want to read—and hopefully buy.

Chapter 21

Everything Works

WRITERS SOMETIMES DON'T INITIALLY BELIEVE ME when I tell them that *every* great story can be broken down into a powerful one-sentence logline. This probably stems from the ongoing misconception that a logline is essentially a one-sentence summary of the plot, which of course it is not. A 300-page novel will never become a single sentence logline with that incorrect assumption. The reason that any piece of material can be broken down into a true logline is because each and every tale has one thing in common: a reliance on the same main three components that appear in a good logline. In fact, the logline has those elements precisely *because* all truly top-notch stories have those exact origins.

At dinner parties, my friends and I sometimes make a game of figuring out the logline for a certain show or film. Usually they are trying to stump me! But there are no exceptions to the fact that any story can be broken down into a solid logline. Below are just a few *very* rough examples I've created from both television and film, scripted and unscripted, both live action and animation, and even a stage play.

Breaking Bad (Fiction Drama TV Series)

A poor chemistry teacher with lung cancer becomes an unlikely meth dealer to secure his family's financial future before he dies.

The Hunger Games (Fiction Feature Film)

In a dystopian future, a girl must survive a government-created "game" where teens kill teens, in order to save her sister's life.

Here Comes Honey Boo Boo (Reality TV)

A child beauty pageant contestant and her outrageous family pick at scab of what's "socially acceptable" while redefining the redneck stereotype.

Les Misérables (Theatrical Musical)

During the French revolution, a prisoner breaks parole and is hunted by a vigilant police inspector.

Sherlock (Fiction Drama TV Series)

A talented but antisocial PI and his physician sidekick solve cases to help an inept police force stop multiple killers.

South Park (Adult Animated Sitcom)

Four young boys, with crude language and dark humor, satirize situations which arise in this fictional Colorado town.

How to Survive a Plague (Nonfiction Feature Film)

Long-unseen amateur footage tells the true story of how advocacy groups responded to the AIDS crisis during the absence of official help.

Twilight (Fiction Feature Film)

A small-town girl puts her life at risk when she falls in love with a boy who turns out to be a vampire.

Duck Dynasty (Reality TV)

A family, known for their uber-long beards and Christian views, becomes stupid rich making products for duck hunters.

X-Men (Fiction Feature Film)

Two men with unique genetic mutations fight on opposing sides, when humans discover the existence of a great many of their kind within the population.

Dancing with the Stars (Television Variety Show)

Past celebrities are paired with professional dancers to compete through a variety of dance styles until one couple is chosen as champion.

The Importance of Being Earnest (Comedy Play)

A man pretends to have a scandalous brother as a cover for his own bad behavior when he's away, but risks losing his love when the ruse is discovered.

How I Met Your Mother (Fiction Comedy TV Series)

A man tells his kids tales of his past love life adventures in NY, while they guess which woman ultimately became their mother.

Room 237 (Nonfiction Feature Film)

An anthology of varying improbable theories shake up the familiar perception of Kubrick's film The Shining.

Captain America (Fiction Feature Film)

A scrawny man is transformed, through a secret government project and serum, into a super-human soldier to stop Nazi attempts at world domination.

Hardcore Pawn (Reality TV)

A family struggles to operate a drama-filled pawn shop in the most dangerous part of Detroit, Michigan.

How to Train Your Dragon (Animated Feature Film)

A young Viking must fight his father's outdated beliefs to prove that Dragons can be friends rather than killers.

Arrow (Fiction TV Series)

A billionaire playboy begins fighting crime as a caped vigilante using only a bow and arrow.

The Simpsons (Animated Comedy TV Series)

A man's basement IQ and screwy family affect his ability to be a good husband and father.

Big (Fiction Feature Film)

A boy's wish to be "big" is granted, but after living as a child trapped in an adult's body and world, he is desperate to return to being a carefree kid.

Survivor (Reality TV Game Show)

A group of marooned strangers must survive, while competing in challenges, in order to become "sole survivor" and win one million dollars.

Romancing the Stone (Fiction Feature Film)

A timid romance writer discovers a priceless emerald and true love when she travels to the jungles of Colombia to save her sister from a madman.

House (Fiction Drama TV Series)

A world-renowned but troubled doctor uses extremely unorthodox methods to solve the most difficult-to-diagnose cases.

Annie (Theatrical Musical)

An orphaned girl is adopted by a wealthy, emotion-phobic man to whom she must teach the true meaning of "family."

The Dr. Oz Show (Television Talk Show)

A doctor known for giving "non-scientific" advice explores medical issues and personal health to help a live audience as well as those at home.

Jurassic Park (Fiction Feature Film)

A scientist travels to a cloned-dinosaur theme park but when the creatures break free from captivity, he must save his family and get them off the island.

As you can see from the examples I've provided above, it doesn't matter whether the product is a drama or comedy, thriller, romance, or action-adventure. Additionally, I purposely chose all different types of media—like animation and reality television—to break down into loglines in order to show that it unequivocally works for everything. You'll also notice that it's unimportant what the overall length of the final show happens to be. It also makes no difference whether the distribution method is television or feature film or theatrical play. Every story can be successfully broken down into one solid, captivating selling sentence. That's what makes a logline so extraordinarily powerful.

Chapter 22

Conclusion

HAVE YOU ALWAYS WANTED TO BRING YOUR WORDS AND ideas to a bigger audience? Have you always believed you had the next great story or screenplay inside, waiting to be set free? This book has presented you with the key to unlocking all of that potential, to letting the rest of the world know—in only one amazing sentence—that you definitely have what everyone else is going to want. You can personally know that your work is the best thing since sliced toast, but if you can't make the rest of the world aware of it, you are doing yourself a disservice.

The art of the logline is really about gaining experience in a process that can lead to incredible opportunity. After all, selling is a way of life. Every day, what we choose to wear sells our personality, how we deal with our bosses sells our skill in handling our jobs, and how we drive sells our credibility to the DMV. At its core, our world truly revolves around marketing. In just the same way, our ability to answer a question about what we are currently working on sells our most important commodity: our creativity.

What good does it do you to write an amazing blockbuster film, cool short story, or even the next best seller if you can't pitch it? I always ask filmmakers about this because many of them, when they are starting out, don't think about distribution. The goal is just "get the movie made." While that's an admirable goal, there's no point in going through the difficulties of packaging, casting, pre-production, production, and post-production only to realize that you haven't set up any kind of delivery system, so no one is going to see your film. In creative industries, as with the rest of the working world, it is—and yes, I know I'm repeating myself—all about selling. And the true gift of a good logline is that it can help you achieve the goal of getting someone (like a potential theatrical distributor, for example) excited about your work.

To me, a logline is like a fabulous culinary experience: Filled with the right ingredients, it can fill you up while simultaneously making you ache for more. It also shows your creative ability and powerful talent. So the impact of being able to craft that influential sentence should not be underestimated. It's come in handy many times during my career of 20-plus years in the entertainment industry.

Recently, I had lunch with an executive with an overall deal at Universal who casually mentioned a need for some male-driven, action-oriented content. At that moment, I was able to rattle off a logline for a new property I'd just been given which fit that bill, and not even a week later, the two of us were developing it with the author—who hadn't even written much yet. She only had a proposal, but it was enough to develop, to take in as a feature film to Universal Pictures. The takeaway from this is that one dynamic sentence, one deceptively simple and very brief pitch, can truly change everything.

So you've read this book and studied both what loglines really are and how to create them successfully—and now it's time to put those new skills to use. I suggest running later drafts of your logline by others who have read your material, to see if they feel it identifies the protagonist, what that person wants, and, of course, what is at stake (as discussed numerous times in the earlier chapters of this book). Overall, does your logline help express the story in a way that encourages interest in reading the query letter and eventually the full manuscript? There is nothing more helpful than gaining a new perspective on your logline by checking it out with others to see if they become engaged and excited by your one-sentence masterpiece or not. After numerous drafts and umpteen revisions, I am often thankful to find someone with fresh eyes to take a peek. That way, I have a new neutral barometer on how the logline is working—or not working, as the case may be. Don't underestimate the worth of new eyes with a new perspective.

Throughout this book, you've learned a great deal of information that will provide you with the ammunition you need to sell your story. You've discovered that loglines can help you stay on track as you write your story. This is incredibly valuable, because it can save you hours of rewriting later on down the line. And as someone who writes, you know how helpful it would be to have a few extra hours back in your corner when you need them. Additionally, you've found out that loglines are the ultimate selling tool. They can help you to share your literary masterpiece with agents, editors, publishers, executives, other writers, neighbors, and friends in a way that expresses how unique and dramatic it truly is. What a boon to be able to sell your "baby" with a minimum of muss and fuss to anyone who asks. Most important, you now know that loglines give you the power to answer the question of what your story is about with an engaging sentence that will entice people to give it that first read. And that, my friends, is true success.

For more information and help with loglines, go to *www.SellItInaSentence.com*

Logline Cheat Sheet

1. Write down a logline, even if it's rambling, just to get started.

2. Ask yourself: "Who is the protagonist?"

3. Determine the number of protagonists (one, two, or multiple).

4. Ask: "What does the protagonist want?"

5. Be specific in your answer.

6. Ask: "What is at stake?"

7. Again, ask: "What happens if they don't achieve what they want?"

8. Be specific in your answer.

9. Remind yourself that this can only be one tight sentence.

10. Make sure to cut names.

11. Make sure to cut ages.

12. Make sure to cut unnecessary adjectives and unneeded words.

13. Check that you are using active rather than passive voice.

14. Finesse: use better vocabulary and make any final tweaks or edits.

15. Share your logline with others—are they are excited by your story?

16. If not, revise it again.

17. If so, memorize your logline.

18. Sell your story in a single sentence.

Logline Samples
& Explanations

These are rough draft loglines taken directly from some of my own projects. They will give you a strong sense of what works and why.

1. *An African American woman uses magical powder to appear white, but when she discovers it's made with arsenic she hunts for the creator to stop people from dying.*

The descriptive "African American" is left in intentionally, as it is vital to the plot of the story. Also, "magical" is necessary to let you know that there is a fantasy element in the book. Notice, as well, that the woman doesn't "look" for the creator, she "hunts" for him. This makes the logline more active and dynamic.

2. *A man discovers an unusual emerald, not realizing that its powers will erase the memories of all who touch it.*

In the book, it's actually the world's largest emerald, and for a time, that was listed as the beginning of the logline. But as it was rewritten again and again, I asked myself how vital that really was to the story. Nifty, yes—but vital? No. Slowly, I realized that it wasn't as important as the fact that the emerald had unusual properties, since that was the element moving the action forward. Once that was clarified, suddenly, the rest of the logline fell into place.

3. *A reporter is convinced that an old age home owner is killing her residents, and puts his own life in danger to prove it.*

The writer was under the impression that the old age home owner was the protagonist, and the original logline reflected that. But it's the reporter's investigation that drives the story forward, and the risk of him getting killed in the process is what's at stake. An earlier draft ended with ". . . trying to prove it," but in the active voice of a logline, you don't try—you do. So the word "trying" was cut out of this later version.

4. *A debutante learns that only by helping those she wronged in life can she ascend to heaven after her death.*

Why "debutante" instead of "girl"? In this situation, it's the character's own selfish, spoiled actions that seal her fate; they affect everything that happens to her in the story. So it was important to emphasize the kind of person she is, and that word became the easiest way to do so without a lot of unnecessary description (which was in previous drafts of the logline).

5. *An elf who can reanimate animals is kidnapped by a wizard who steals her abilities and awakens griffins, the killers of elves.*

This was a very complicated fantasy story, filled with dragons, gold, fairies, magic, warlocks, and many other elements. The writer was desperate to figure out how to create a logline with so much going on in the book. Only by boiling the plot down to its basic components—who is the protagonist? (the elf); what is his/her journey? (to escape her kidnapper); what is at stake? (the death of all elves if she fails)—did the logline finally become clear.

6. *A slacker teen decides to run for mayor in order to get the girl and, to everyone's surprise, he wins.*

It was important to make clear here the exact reason the teen ran for mayor, because that specifies what the protagonist wants. Let me clarify: He doesn't want to run for mayor; he wants to impress a hot chick who's in his class, which ends in his half-baked idea to run for mayor. And what's at stake? Well, now he has to follow through and actually be the mayor!

7. *An author uses her friends' lives as book fodder and accidentally creates a best seller that threatens to ruin her relationships with them.*

The toughest thing here was concentrating on only the one protagonist, because in the book, all four women are given equal time and equal weight. In fact, each chapter is told by a different woman in the group. That said, it was the woman whose actions (in writing the truth-based book) affected everyone else, which kept the story moving along at its fast and furious pace. So it became clear that she needed to be the focus of the logline.

8. *A nice kid who's a crappy superhero decides he'll be an awesome villain instead, but struggles since he isn't wired to be mean.*

This was such a cute concept that it was important to me to choose vocabulary that reflected that tone, hence my use of words like "crappy" and "awesome," adjectives which I would normally cut. I even ended up keeping the word "nice," because I felt it helped explain why the kid would have trouble being a villain and wasn't "wired to be mean."

9. *A dog trainer finds the lessons she uses on her animals work even better on the men she dates.*

This is a nonfiction/memoir property for which I helped the writer twist her occupation to create a hook, which ultimately helped her write a more unique piece about her dating experiences. That's why you always write the logline early in your creation process, before you write the entire manuscript—I just can't stress that enough.

10. *Young twins use their sleuthing skills to become the go-to gals for solving cold cases, which continually puts them in hot water.*

Here is an unusual two-protagonist example, which I brought up earlier in this book. There are essentially dual protagonists here, because the girls are identical twins who affect the story 100 percent equally throughout. I also decided that it would be fun to keep the general "hot water," because even though it's not specific, it plays off of the "cold cases" they solve.

11. *A counselor runs a camp for adults with marital problems, but is stuck repairing the marriage of a woman he's in love with.*

This is another example where the stakes are already built in, because it's essentially a Romeo and Juliet logline. These two can't be together because it's his job to help the woman get back together with her husband—so it doesn't matter that he's in love with her. The two of them getting together would pose innumerable issues because of the situation itself.

12. *An inventor's daughter witnesses her father's kidnapping and must employ his own inventions to rescue him from kidnappers determined to use his latest creation to destroy mankind.*

This is a good example of establishing the protagonist (the inventor's daughter), what she wants (to rescue her father), and what's at stake (if she doesn't succeed, the bad guys get to use his inventions for evil). The interesting thing is that the content creator thought the father was the protagonist initially, because he was the one who was kidnapped, but I showed him that the daughter makes all of the decisions from that point on. Her father's kidnapping was what we call the "inciting incident:" just the initial event that sets everything in motion.

13. *A socialite is stranded with a curmudgeonly backwoodsman during a snowstorm and must change herself into a decent person before he forces her to wait out the blizzard in the barn.*

Normally, I would have immediately cut out the adjective "curmudgeonly," but in this instance I left it in because I felt that otherwise the stakes weren't high enough. I didn't think you would ever believe that the woodsman would actually throw her out to spend the night with the animals if you didn't first get a sense of what kind of person he was. I also changed "nice" to "decent," because anyone can fake being nice but it's much harder to actually become a decent human being. Once again, it raised the stakes.

14. *A lawyer must become a detective when confidentiality prevents him from telling police about murders before they happen, which he thinks his client is committing.*

In most cases, I'd immediately change "which he thinks his client is committing" to "which his client is committing," because it has more power. However, I realized that it's actually the uncertainty—the question of whether or not his client is doing the killings—that makes this story so intriguing. Because of that fact, I didn't want to lose that neat morsel of doubt within the logline.

15. *A mortician's assistant questions her sanity when the dead start talking to her, but ultimately puts her life at risk to help the deceased fix injustices so they can rest in peace.*

Originally, I cut out the beginning about the dead talking to her and just had the logline say that a mortician's assistant put her life at risk to help the deceased fix injustices . . . but it suddenly seemed strange that she was helping the dead. How was she helping the dead if they were dead, right? Also, it was a bit confusing when there was no information about how she'd know the deceased had problems that needed to be rectified in the first place—so the first part ended up back in the logline. It's one thing to cut words because the logline has a cost of ten dollars per word. It's another to perplex your reader due to a lack of important information.

In the examples above, you can see the application of all we have learned throughout this book. While they may need a bit of further finessing, these loglines are tight, intriguing, and present all of the answers to the main questions of who the protagonist is, what they desire, and what is at stake if they don't get what they want/need.

Now it's time to see if you've really learned all this book had to teach you. You need to put into practice every bit of knowledge you've gained so that you can create loglines for your own work. In the next section I've included ten basic practice loglines to get you started as well as twenty more complex practice loglines to challenge you, along with separate answer pages. See how you do. Here's the chance to really appreciate how much you've absorbed!

Workbook— Simple Loglines

Here are some simple loglines to begin with, to help you begin to apply all that you have learned in this book. As a jumping off point, see if you can decide what to cut in order to end up with a fairly decent logline.

1. George, an ambitious but misguided bartender, inherits his father Jamie's rundown tavern just as the town bans alcohol, so he must set up a bootlegging ring to make money or die destitute.

2. Famous actor Justin Tate uses advice taken from all of his rom-com films in order to help an uber-fan named Henry find true love, but problems arise when he falls for the same girl, and both movie life and real life begin to blur.

3. John Jacobs is a lowly employee stuck on his company's motivational camping trip, which is boring, but it suddenly turns into a life-and-death struggle when he discovers that his nasty boss, Kevin Carson, is actually a killer.

4. An aging 80-plus-year-old man discovers that his sickly wife truly believes the only way she can be happy with her impending demise is that she must take her husband with her into death, and so he must find a way to stop her before she succeeds in killing them both together.

5. A dragon, a troll, and a fairy are all fairy-tale creatures stuck in a magical land, and they decide that they must go on a quest to see what's in the outside world, but find that their powers are useless out there and in fact they return changed into simple human beings, which makes them outcasts.

6. After her sweet single mother drowns, a high school senior girl becomes more determined than ever to become a swim team star in order to fight her inner demons.

7. A quantum physics professor accidentally triggers an explosion that sends him ten years into the past, but then it gets worse when he gets stuck there, and if he doesn't find a way home he knows it will eventually affect time and erase his own existence.

8. Adeline, a retired old woman with 50 felines, is desperate to find homes for them all before she dies and

her mean neighbor calls animal control, but her nasty neighbor ultimately surprises her and helps her and takes in the last cat that has to be placed.

9. A toy store employee locked in the store by accident attempts to rescue a kidnapped Santa Claus who has been taken by cruel, ruthless killers who want to have him save them from prison for Christmas.

10. An African journalist's car breaks down while she is on the way to pursue the greatest story of her career— unfortunately, it's at the only town for miles around, which turns out to be inhabited by cannibals.

Workbook—Simple Logline Answers

1.

ORIGINAL

George, an ambitious but misguided bartender, inherits his father Jamie's rundown tavern just as the town bans alcohol, so he must set up a bootlegging ring to make money or die destitute.

REDO

A ~~George, an ambitious but misguided~~ bartender, inherits his father ~~Jamie~~'s rundown tavern just as the town bans alcohol, so he must set up a bootlegging ring ~~to make money~~ or die destitute.

CLEAN

A bartender inherits his father's rundown tavern just as the town bans alcohol, so he must set up a bootlegging ring or die destitute.

2.

ORIGINAL

Famous actor Justin Tate uses advice taken from all of his rom-com films in order to help an uber-fan named Henry find true love, but problems arise when he falls for the same girl, and both movie life and real life begin to blur.

REDO

A Famous actor ~~Justin Tate~~ uses advice ~~taken~~ from ~~all of~~ his ~~rom-com~~ films ~~in order~~ to help an uber-fan ~~named Henry~~ find ~~true~~ love, but problems arise when he falls for the same girl, ~~and both movie life and real life begin to blur.~~

CLEAN

A famous actor uses advice from his films to help an uber-fan find love, but problems arise when he falls for the same girl.

3.

ORIGINAL

John Jacobs is a lowly employee stuck on his company's motivational camping trip, which is boring, but it suddenly turns into a life-and-death struggle when he discovers that his nasty boss, Kevin Carson, is actually a killer.

REDO

~~John Jacobs is~~ a lowly employee IS stuck on his company's ~~motivational~~ camping trip, which ~~is boring, but it suddenly~~ turns into a life-and-death struggle when he discovers ~~that~~ his ~~nasty~~ boss, ~~Kevin Carson,~~ is ~~actually~~ a killer.

CLEAN

A lowly employee is stuck on his company's camping trip, which turns into a life-and-death struggle when he discovers his boss is a killer.

4.

ORIGINAL

An aging 80-plus-year-old man discovers that his sickly wife truly believes the only way she can be happy with her impending demise is that she must take her husband with her into death, and so he must find a way to stop her before she succeeds in killing them both together.

REDO

An aging 80-plus-year-old man discovers that his sickly wife truly believes the only way she can be happy with her impending demise is that she must take her husband with her into death, and so he must find a way to stop her before she succeeds in killing them both together.

CLEAN

A man discovers his sickly wife believes she must take her husband with her into death, and so must find a way to stop her.

5.

ORIGINAL

A dragon, a troll, and a fairy are all fairy-tale creatures stuck in a magical land, and they decide that they must go on a quest to see what's in the outside world, but find that their powers are useless out there and in fact they return changed into simple human beings, which makes them outcasts.

REDO

~~A dragon, a troll, and a fairy are all~~ fairy-tale creatures ~~stuck in a magical land, and they~~ decide ~~that~~ they must ~~go on a quest to~~ see what's in the outside world, but ~~find that their powers are useless out there and in fact they~~ return changed into simple human beings, which makes them outcasts.

CLEAN

Fairy-tale creatures decide they must see what's in the outside world but return changed into simple human beings, which makes them outcasts.

6.

ORIGINAL

After her sweet single mother drowns, a high school senior girl becomes more determined than ever to become a swim team star in order to fight her inner demons.

REDO

After her ~~sweet single~~ mother drowns, a ~~high school senior~~ girl becomes ~~more~~ determined ~~than ever~~ to become a swim ~~team~~ star ~~in order to fight her inner demons.~~

CLEAN

After her mother drowns, a girl becomes determined to become a swim star.

7.

ORIGINAL

A quantum physics professor accidentally triggers an explosion that sends him ten years into the past, but then it gets worse when he gets stuck there, and if he doesn't find a way home he knows it will eventually affect time and erase his own existence.

REDO

A ~~quantum physics~~ professor accidentally ~~triggers an explosion that~~ sends himSELF ~~ten years~~ into the past, ~~but then it gets worse when he gets stuck there,~~ and if he doesn't find a way home ~~he knows~~ it will eventually ~~affect time and~~ erase his ~~own~~ existence.

CLEAN

A professor accidentally sends himself into the past, and if he doesn't find a way home it will eventually erase his existence.

8.

ORIGINAL

Adeline, a retired old woman with 50 felines, is desperate to find homes for them all before she dies and her mean neighbor calls animal control, but her nasty neighbor ultimately surprises her and helps her and takes in the last cat that has to be placed.

REDO

~~Adeline,~~ a ~~retired old~~ woman with 50 ~~felines,~~ is desperate to find homes for them ~~all~~ before she dies ~~and~~ WHEN ~~her mean neighbor calls animal control, but~~ her nasty neighbor ~~ultimately~~ surprises her and ~~helps her and~~ takes in the last cat ~~that has to be placed~~.

CLEAN

A woman with 50 felines is desperate to find homes for them before she dies when her nasty neighbor surprises her and takes in the last cat.

9.

ORIGINAL

A toy store employee locked in the store by accident attempts to rescue a kidnapped Santa Claus who has been taken by cruel, ruthless killers who want to have him save them from prison for Christmas.

REDO

A toy store employee ~~locked in the store by accident~~ attempts to rescue a kidnapped Santa ~~Claus who has been taken by cruel, ruthless killers~~ AND ~~who want to have him~~ save ~~them from prison for~~ Christmas.

CLEAN

A toy store employee attempts to rescue a kidnapped Santa and save Christmas.

10.

ORIGINAL

An African journalist's car breaks down while she is on the way to pursue the greatest story of her career—unfortunately, it's at the only town for miles around, which turns out to be inhabited by cannibals.

REDO

An ~~African~~ journalist's car breaks down ~~while she is on the way to pursue the greatest story of her career— unfortunately, it's~~ at the only town ~~for miles around, which turns out to be~~ inhabited by cannibals.

CLEAN

A journalist's car breaks down at the only town inhabited by cannibals.

How did you do? Do you think you're ready for a more difficult challenge? If so, I've compiled a list of more difficult loglines in the next section. Again, they are rough, needing further finessing, but they should still provide an adequate test for those of you who want to challenge yourselves a bit more.

Workbook—
Complex Loglines

Here are some more complicated sample loglines to try out at home. These will end up as true rough drafts, loglines to be further refined with dynamic vocabulary and the like, but they will help you continue to learn the process.

1. Guided by conflicting motives, a queen and a peasant must venture on a quest to retrieve and recapture a magical bird that escaped from the czar's menagerie. If they do not succeed, she'll be forced to marry the first man who does capture the bird.

2. The Vietnam War turned some people into savages while others found their moral compass. When a US Navy officer who has a burning need to prove himself and a beautiful Indian woman who is collaborating with the Vietcong fall in love in grim 1964 Saigon, they are each forced to make decisions about who they are and what is important to them, and must defect or lose each other forever.

3. Framed through the lens of collegiate fraternity and sorority life, the story features two friends as they

struggle to unearth their own identities and fall in love, ultimately succumbing to the reality that their deepest desires are no match for cruel twists of fate when they then find out that they are actually brother and sister.

4. Set in ancient Egypt, this is the story of a common Egyptian trying to hold his family together while facing the impending Hebrew exodus, and who ultimately discovers his true love and must save her life while receiving salvation as the plagues fall one by one from the mysterious hand of a God unknown.

5. Amanda Bixby begins to escape debilitating depression when she becomes a woman with an obsession with a serial killer, Gregory Hennes. Their intimate correspondence leads to a death-row wedding, after which Amanda begins to face the truth about Greg even while she puts her mental health at risk from his manic episodes.

6. In a creature-filled universe where Valkyries, werewolves, and ogres roam, a 13-year-old young human girl, mistaken for a sprite, struggles to survive long enough to find a way back to her own world.

7. After 50 years, a viper, Amelia Tooley, finally finds another one of her kind . . . who is determined to kill her and abduct her child, so Amelia determines that she must either save her child, whom she loves, or kill

him before he can be used by the other viper to destroy the world.

8. An unlikely team of a private investigator and a maid must work together to uncover a clandestine plot and learn why the city's ruling council is blocking their investigation, while at the same time stop those determined to unearth an ancient library that is filled only with unbelievably dangerous books on deadly black magic.

9. Thomas Bean, a young, naive, hopeful aspiring journalist who relocates to the US from London to follow his passion and put a painful past behind him, finds himself investigating a grisly murder, which puts him on the brink of a deadlier mystery on both sides of the Atlantic as he fights to expose an international crime ring, which involves trafficking in sterilized women, and puts his own life in extreme peril while doing so.

10. When the police rule three dead women as accidents, a lazy Hawaiian PI, Charlie Ho, teams up with an uptight female Boston journalist to track down a serial killer whose weapons of choice involve various uses for poisonous animals in order to immobilize his prey.

11. Dr. Jonathan Hartley's past and present are on a rapid collision course, a battle transpiring within the forces of fate and destiny that haunt us all, as he navigates the unpredictable labyrinth of life-threatening illness while deciding whether or not to marry his fiancée.

12. When 16-year-old Amanda Williams earns a scholarship and fulfills a dream to study abroad in Spain, she leaves her life as a poor, friendless orphan behind but finds herself tangled in an inescapable world of dark magic as she fights becoming a demon.

13. Identical 15-year-old twin boys embark on a quest as they vow to swap 25 souls with the devil in exchange for the return of their grandfather, who has been abducted down to hell and stuck there by an evil curse of magic.

14. A true-story thriller that follows the life of FBI Agent Travers as he enters a world of mystery and intrigue in locations such as the Bahamas—as the clock winds down, Travers follows clues, while undercover, which take him on an amazing journey to stop an international diamond-smuggling operation and get out with his life.

15. Jay, a crass, backwater attorney, stumbles out of the whorehouse and then races to save a young boy's life while also narrowly avoiding disbarment by outsmarting a slick policeman who he truly believes is committing and then solving his very own crimes.

16. A young, idealistic, and somewhat naive oil painter and all-around artist risks her hard-won career to expose a museum's deep, dark, secret conspiracy regarding the swapping out of masterpieces with forgeries over four decades.

17. A dying con man attempts to reconnect with his estranged daughter, Ella, whom he never knew, but instead of fixing what is wrong with their relationship he ends up forced to draft her to help him in his last sting, which involves the mob (pissed off at him for a previous job gone wrong), but what surprises them both is they learn to love each other during the ensuing escapade.

18. Marigold travels back in time to get multiple opportunities to try to trick fate and win Marcus, the man of her dreams, but she soon realizes that in order to have a chance at a happy ending she needs to wait until he falls in love with her all on his own—even if that never happens and she loses him forever.

19. Liz Anson, a coldly calculating professional assassin, has been assigned to kill Charles Unger, a nosy investigative reporter who's gotten much too close to an evil genetics corporation, but she is unable to bring herself to pull the trigger because she is as desperately in love with her target as he is with her, and it's a recipe for disaster.

20. A genetically engineered cyborg teen and her equally mechanical friends who are also cyborgs are tasked with saving what is left of humanity, which is basically just a young couple with a baby on the way, after the scientists who created the cyborgs accidentally set off the apocalypse.

Workbook—Complex Logline Answers

How did you do?

1.

ORIGINAL

Guided by conflicting motives, a queen and a peasant must venture on a quest to retrieve and recapture a magical bird that escaped from the czar's menagerie. If they do not succeed, she'll be forced to marry the first man who does capture the bird.

REDO

~~Guided by conflicting motives,~~ a queen ~~and a peasant~~ must ~~venture on a quest to retrieve and~~ recapture a magical bird ~~that escaped from the czar's menagerie. If they do not succeed, she'll~~ OR be forced to marry the first man who does ~~capture the bird~~.

CLEAN

A queen must recapture a magical bird or be forced to marry the first man who does.

2.

ORIGINAL

The Vietnam War turned some people into savages while others found their moral compass. When a US Navy officer who has a burning need to prove himself and a beautiful Indian woman who is collaborating with the Vietcong fall in love in grim 1964 Saigon, they are each forced to make decisions about who they are and what is important to them, and must defect or lose each other forever.

REDO

~~The Vietnam War turned some people into savages while others found their moral compass.~~ When a US ~~Navy~~ officer ~~who has a burning need to prove himself~~ and aN ~~beautiful~~ Indian woman ~~who is~~ collaborating with the Vietcong fall in love ~~in grim 1964 Saigon,~~ they are ~~each~~ forced to ~~make decisions about who they are and what is important to them, and must~~ defect or lose each other forever.

CLEAN

When a US officer and an Indian woman collaborating with the Vietcong fall in love, they are forced to defect or lose each other forever.

3.

ORIGINAL

Framed through the lens of collegiate fraternity and sorority life, the story features two friends as they struggle to unearth their own identities and fall in love, ultimately succumbing to the reality that their deepest desires are no match for cruel twists of fate when they then find out that they are actually brother and sister.

REDO

~~Framed through the lens of~~ collegiate ~~fraternity and sorority life, the story features two~~ friends ~~as they struggle to unearth their own identities and~~ fall in love, ~~ultimately succumbing to the reality that their deepest desires are no match for cruel twists of fate when they~~ then find out that they are actually brother and sister.

CLEAN

Collegiate friends fall in love, then find out that they are actually brother and sister.

4.

ORIGINAL

Set in ancient Egypt, this is the story of a common Egyptian trying to hold his family together while facing the impending Hebrew exodus, and who ultimately discovers his true love and must save her life while receiving salvation as the plagues fall one by one from the mysterious hand of a God unknown.

REDO

~~Set in ancient Egypt, this is the story of~~ aN ~~common~~ Egyptian ~~trying to hold his family together while~~ facing the impending Hebrew exodus~~, and who ultimately~~ discovers his true love and must save her life ~~while receiving salvation~~ as the plagues fall ~~one by one from the mysterious hand of a God unknown.~~

CLEAN

An Egyptian facing the impending Hebrew exodus discovers his true love and must save her life as the plagues fall.

5.

ORIGINAL

Amanda Bixby begins to escape debilitating depression when she becomes a woman with an obsession with a serial killer, Gregory Hennes. Their intimate correspondence leads to a death-row wedding, after which Amanda begins to face the truth about Greg even while she puts her mental health at risk from his manic episodes.

REDO

~~Amanda Bixby begins to escape debilitating depression when she becomes~~ a woman'S ~~with an~~ obsession with a serial killer, ~~Gregory Hennes. Their intimate correspon-~~ ~~dence~~ leads to a death-row wedding, ~~after~~ which ~~Amanda~~ ~~begins to face the truth about Greg even while she~~ puts her mental health at risk from his manic episodes.

CLEAN

A woman's obsession with a serial killer leads to a death-row wedding, which puts her mental health at risk from his manic episodes.

6.

ORIGINAL

In a creature-filled universe where Valkyries, werewolves, and ogres roam, a 13-year-old young human girl, mistaken for a sprite, struggles to survive long enough to find a way back to her own world.

REDO

In a creature-filled universe ~~where Valkyries, werewolves,~~ ~~and ogres roam,~~ a ~~13-year-old young human~~ girl, mistaken for a sprite, struggles to survive ~~long enough~~ and find a way back to her ~~own~~ world.

CLEAN

In a creature-filled universe, a girl mistaken for a sprite struggles to survive and find a way back to her world.

7.

ORIGINAL

After 50 years, a viper, Amelia Tooley, finally finds another one of her kind . . . who is determined to kill her and abduct her child, so Amelia determines that she must either save her child, whom she loves, or kill him before he can be used by the other viper to destroy the world.

REDO

~~After 50 years,~~ a viper~~, Amelia Tooley, finally finds another one of her kind . . . who is determined to kill her and abduct her child, so Amelia determines that she~~ must either save her child~~, whom she loves,~~ or kill him before he can be used by ~~the~~ ANother viper to destroy the world.

CLEAN

A viper must either save her child or kill him before he can be used by another viper to destroy the world.

8.

ORIGINAL

An unlikely team of a private investigator and a maid must work together to uncover a clandestine plot and learn why the city's ruling council is blocking their investigation, while at the same time stop those determined to unearth an ancient library that is filled only with unbelievably dangerous books on deadly black magic.

REDO

~~An unlikely team of~~ a private investigator and a maid must ~~work together to uncover a clandestine plot and learn why the city's ruling council is blocking their investigation, while at the same time~~ stop those determined to unearth an ancient library ~~that is~~ filled ~~only~~ with ~~unbelievably dangerous~~ books on deadly black magic.

CLEAN

A private investigator and a maid must stop those determined to unearth an ancient library filled with books on deadly black magic.

9.

ORIGINAL

Thomas Bean, a young, naive, hopeful aspiring journalist who relocates to the US from London to follow his passion and put a painful past behind him, finds himself investigating a grisly murder, which puts him on the brink of a deadlier mystery on both sides of the Atlantic as he fights to expose an international crime ring, which involves trafficking in sterilized women, and puts his own life in extreme peril while doing so.

REDO

~~Thomas Bean,~~ a ~~young~~ naïve ~~hopeful~~ aspiring journalist ~~who relocates to the US from London to follow his passion and put a painful past behind him, finds himself investigating a grisly murder, which puts him on the brink of a~~

~~deadlier mystery on both sides of the Atlantic as he~~ fights to expose an international crime ring~~, which involves~~ trafficking in sterilized women, ~~and~~ WHICH puts his own life in ~~extreme~~ peril ~~while doing so.~~

CLEAN

A naive aspiring journalist fights to expose an international crime ring, trafficking in sterilized women, which puts his own life in peril.

10.

ORIGINAL

When the police rule three dead women as accidents, a lazy Hawaiian PI, Charlie Ho, teams up with an uptight female Boston journalist to track down a serial killer whose weapons of choice involve various uses for poisonous animals in order to immobilize his prey.

REDO

~~When the police rule three dead women as accidents,~~ a lazy Hawaiian PI~~, Charlie Ho,~~ teams ~~up~~ with an uptight ~~female~~ Boston journalist to track ~~down~~ a ~~serial~~ killer who~~se weapons of choice involve various~~ uses ~~for~~ poisonous animals ~~in order~~ to immobilize his prey.

CLEAN

A lazy Hawaiian PI teams with an uptight Boston journalist to track a killer who uses poisonous animals to immobilize his prey.

11.

ORIGINAL

Dr. Jonathan Hartley's past and present are on a rapid collision course, a battle transpiring within the forces of fate and destiny that haunt us all, as he navigates the unpredictable labyrinth of life-threatening illness while deciding whether or not to marry his fiancée.

REDO

A DOCTOR ~~Dr. Jonathan Hartley's past and present are on a rapid collision course, a battle transpiring within the forces of fate and destiny that haunt us all, as he~~ navigates the ~~unpredictable~~ labyrinth of HIS OWN life-threatening illness while deciding whether ~~or not~~ to marry his fiancée.

CLEAN

A doctor navigates the labyrinth of his own life-threatening illness while deciding whether to marry his fiancée.

12.

ORIGINAL

When 16-year-old Amanda Williams earns a scholarship and fulfills a dream to study abroad in Spain, she leaves her life as a poor, friendless orphan behind but finds herself tangled in an inescapable world of dark magic as she fights becoming a demon.

REDO

~~When 16-year-old Amanda Williams earns a scholarship and~~ A STUDENT fulfills a dream to study ~~abroad~~ in Spain~~, she leaves her life as a poor, friendless orphan behind~~ but finds herself tangled in ~~an inescapable~~ A world of dark magic FIGHTING ~~as she fights~~ becoming a demon.

CLEAN

A student fulfills a dream to study in Spain but finds herself in a world of dark magic, fighting becoming a demon.

13.

ORIGINAL

Identical 15-year-old twin boys embark on a quest as they vow to swap 25 souls with the devil in exchange for the return of their grandfather, who has been abducted down to hell and stuck there by an evil curse of magic.

REDO

~~Identical 15-year-old~~ twin boys ~~embark on a quest as they~~ vow to swap 25 souls with the devil in exchange for the return of their ABDUCTED grandfather, who ~~has been abducted down to~~ IS STUCK IN hell ~~and stuck there by an evil curse of magic.~~

CLEAN

Twin boys vow to swap 25 souls with the devil in exchange for the return of their abducted grandfather, who is stuck in hell.

14.

ORIGINAL

A true-story thriller that follows the life of FBI Agent Travers as he enters a world of mystery and intrigue in locations such as the Bahamas—as the clock winds down, Travers follows clues, while undercover, which take him on an amazing journey to stop an international diamond-smuggling operation and get out with his life.

REDO

A true-story ~~thriller that follows the life of~~ AN UNDERCOVER FBI Agent ~~Travers as he enters a world of mystery and intrigue in locations such as the Bahamas—as the clock winds down, Travers follows clues, while undercover, which take him on an amazing journey~~ STRIVES to stop an international diamond-smuggling operation and get out with his life.

CLEAN

A true story, an undercover FBI agent strives to stop an international diamond-smuggling operation and get out with his life.

15.

ORIGINAL

Jay, a crass, backwater attorney, stumbles out of the whorehouse and then races to save a young boy's life while also narrowly avoiding disbarment by outsmarting a slick policeman who he truly believes is committing and then solving his very own crimes.

REDO

~~Jay,~~ a ~~crass,~~ backwater attorney~~, stumbles out of the whorehouse and then~~ races to ~~save a young boy's life while also narrowly~~ avoiding disbarment by outsmarting a slick policeman who ~~he truly believes~~ is committing ~~and~~ then solving his ~~very~~ own crimes.

CLEAN

A backwater attorney races to avoid disbarment by outsmarting a slick policeman who is committing then solving his own crimes.

16.

ORIGINAL

A young, idealistic, and somewhat naive oil painter and all-around artist risks her hard-won career to expose a museum's deep, dark, secret conspiracy regarding the swapping out of masterpieces with forgeries over four decades.

REDO

AN ~~young, idealistic, and somewhat naive oil painter and all-around~~ artist risks her ~~hard-won~~ career to expose a museum's ~~deep, dark,~~ secret ~~conspiracy regarding the~~ swapping ~~out~~ of masterpieces with forgeries FOR ~~over four~~ decades.

CLEAN

An artist risks her career to expose a museum's secret swapping of masterpieces with forgeries for decades.

17.

ORIGINAL

A dying con man attempts to reconnect with his estranged daughter, Ella, whom he never knew, but instead of fixing what is wrong with their relationship he ends up forced to draft her to help him in his last sting, which involves the mob (pissed off at him for a previous job gone wrong), but what surprises them both is they learn to love each other during the ensuing escapade.

REDO

A dying con man ~~attempts to~~ reconnectS with his estranged daughter~~, Ella, whom he never knew,~~ but ~~instead of fixing what is wrong with their relationship he ends up~~ IS forced to draft her ~~to help him~~ inTO his last sting, ~~which involves the mob (pissed off at him for a previous job gone~~

~~wrong), but what surprises them both is~~ YET they learn to love each other during the ~~ensuing~~ escapade.

CLEAN

A dying con man reconnects with his estranged daughter but is forced to draft her into his last sting, yet they learn to love each other during the escapade.

18.

ORIGINAL

Marigold travels back in time to get multiple opportunities to try to trick fate and win Marcus, the man of her dreams, but she soon realizes that in order to have a chance at a happy ending she needs to wait until he falls in love with her all on his own—even if that never happens and she loses him forever.

REDO

~~Marigold~~ A WOMAN travels back in time to ~~get multiple opportunities to try to~~ trick fate and win ~~Marcus,~~ the man of her dreams, but ~~she~~ soon realizes ~~that in order to have a chance at a happy ending~~ she ~~needs to~~ MUST wait until he falls in love with her ~~all~~ on his own—~~even if that never happens and she~~ OR loses him forever.

CLEAN

A woman travels back in time to trick fate and win the man of her dreams, but soon realizes she must wait until he falls in love with her on his own or lose him forever.

19.

ORIGINAL

Liz Anson, a coldly calculating professional assassin, has been assigned to kill Charles Unger, a nosy investigative reporter who's gotten much too close to an evil genetics corporation, but she is unable to bring herself to pull the trigger because she is as desperately in love with her target as he is with her, and it's a recipe for disaster.

REDO

~~Liz Anson,~~ a ~~coldly calculating~~ professional assassin~~, has been~~ IS assigned to kill ~~Charles Unger,~~ aN ~~nosy~~ investigative reporter ~~who's gotten much too close to an evil genetics corporation,~~ but ~~she is unable to bring herself to~~ CAN'T pull the trigger because she is as desperately in love with her target as he is with her~~, and it's a recipe for disaster~~.

CLEAN

A professional assassin is assigned to kill an investigative reporter but can't pull the trigger because she is as desperately in love with her target as he is with her.

20.

ORIGINAL

A genetically engineered cyborg teen and her equally mechanical friends who are also cyborgs are tasked with saving what is left of humanity, which is basically just a young couple with a baby on the way, after the scientists who created the cyborgs accidentally set off the apocalypse.

REDO

A ~~genetically engineered~~ cyborg teen and her ~~equally mechanical~~ friends ~~who are also cyborgs are tasked with~~ MUST savE~~ing~~ what is left of humanity, ~~which is basically just~~ a young couple with a baby ~~on the way~~, after ~~the~~ scientists ~~who created the cyborgs~~ accidentally set off the apocalypse.

CLEAN

A cyborg teen and her friends must save what is left of humanity, a young couple with a baby, after scientists accidentally set off the apocalypse.

How did you do in this challenging section? If you are feeling good about what you did on your own for at least half of the logline examples, pat yourself on the back. These are not easy.

Now that this book is at an end, how can you continue your logline education? Do what I did in an earlier chapter: pick novels, TV shows, plays, and films that interest you, and see if you can design a nice, solid selling sentence for it. I promise that the more you practice logline creation, as with anything in life, the better you get at it, and the easier doing it becomes.

Acknowledgments

I'D LIKE TO START BY THANKING THE BRAVE SOULS who have not only attended my lectures and seminars but who had the courage to stand up and read out their desperately-needs-help loglines in front of everyone else. Some of you may recognize yourselves in this book, and I just want to acknowledge and applaud you for both your fearlessness and your impressive commitment to making your work the best it can be.

In addition, I also could not have written this book without the ongoing support of my husband, Andrew Bishop, who basically took over the rest of my life for me during the times when I had to stop everything else and just focus on getting words on paper. It's not something I take lightly because I always have a ridiculous number of other things going on—yet somehow, he handled it all flawlessly. I am incredibly grateful for all you do for me, Andy—and now it's in writing, for you to reference when I forget to say it out loud.

I'd also like to acknowledge my good friend and amazing

agent, Katharine Sands, at the Sarah Jane Freymann Literary Agency, who truly brought *Sell Your Story in a Single Sentence* to life. She'd seen my workshop about how to create a perfect logline and believed that with all of the information I was giving out, a book could be born. And after I delivered, she worked tirelessly to find the perfect publisher for my material. Saying "thank you" seems incredibly inadequate, especially now when it's coming to full-blown fruition, but I am so grateful to Katharine for being the tenacious, encouraging, and creative lady that she is. I am lucky to have her in my corner.

Thank yous should also go to my editor, Ann Treistman, as well as Becca Kaplan, Sarah Bennett, and Devorah Backman at W. W. Norton & Co., who all supported this book in unimaginable ways.

Finally, thank you to Melissa Biederman, my brother Bret Shefter, and my parents Joy and Milt Shefter who are always cheering me on, even when they think I am piling too much on my plate. A support system like that is truly worth its weight in gold.

About the Author

Touted by CNN's iReport as "The Book Whisperer," Lane Shefter Bishop is the CEO of Vast Entertainment. Vast is a book-to-screen adaptation company with numerous television and film projects in development at various networks and studios, including NBCUniversal, Disney/ABC Television Group, CBS, Lifetime, Sony, and 20th Century Fox. All of these projects have one thing in common—they began with a single sentence, a top-notch logline.

To date, Ms. Bishop has been a featured speaker at the Writers Guild of America, the Romantic Times Convention, Romance Writers of America, Writers Boot Camp, The Next Bestseller, Heather Graham's Writers for New Orleans, Women in Film, Grub Street's Muse & the Marketplace, Backspace, ScriptDC, and the London Book Fair.